Arthur Gr Butler

**On a Collection of Lepidoptera made in British East Africa by Mr.**

**C. S. Betton**

Arthur Gr Butler

**On a Collection of Lepidoptera made in British East Africa by Mr. C. S. Betton**

ISBN/EAN: 9783741131721

Manufactured in Europe, USA, Canada, Australia, Japa

Cover: Foto ©Thomas Meinert / pixelio.de

Manufactured and distributed by brebook publishing software
(www.brebook.com)

Arthur Gr Butler

# On a Collection of Lepidoptera made in British East Africa by Mr.

## C. S. Betton

## 2. On a Collection of Lepidoptera made in British East Africa by Mr. C. S. Betton. By ARTHUR G. BUTLER, Ph.D., F.L.S., F.Z.S., &c., Senior Assistant-Keeper, Zoological Department, British Museum.

[Received April 21, 1898.]

(Plates XXXII. & XXXIII.)

Mr. Betton's collection is a singularly interesting one, rich in rare and new species, three Butterflies and twenty-six Moths from the present series being now described for the first time. Among the Butterflies also I may call attention to a suite of *Acræa chilo*, females of *A. crystallina*, the wet-season forms of both *Teracolus hetæra* and *T. puniceus*, the dry form of *T. leo*, a number of examples of *T. venata*, and an example of the rare *Alæna picata*, a species new to the Museum collection.

Although Mr. Betton desired to retain a collection for his private use, yet he sanctioned the whole of the types of new species, and examples of all species needed to perfect the National collection, being retained. Among the Heterocerous Lepidoptera, many of which were only represented by single specimens, he has thus suffered somewhat severely in the interests of science; but in the Butterflies there was considerably less required in proportion to the numbers collected.

Mr. Betton's line of march extended from Mombasa in a north-westerly direction by way of Samburu, Taru, Voi, and Ndi to Tsavo[1]. He has furnished the following notes on the weather prevailing at certain dates between March 1896 and August 1897, during which time his collection was made :—

### 1896.

March 1st–20th.   Slight rain.
May 1st, " greater " rains commence ; May 11th–13th, heavy and continuous rain ; May 13th to end of month, slight rain.
June 21st–27th.   Slight rain.
October 24th.   Rains (" lesser ") commence.
November 1st–15th.   Heavy and continuous rains : rain nearly every day to end of month.
December.   Showers nearly all the month.

### 1897.

February 18th–20th.   Storms.
March 3rd, 4th, and 18th.   Storms.
April 3rd and 4th.   Storms.
April 14th–22nd.   Slight rains.
May 16th–23rd.   Slight rains.
July 8th and 9th.   Heavy showers.
August 10th to 22nd.   Slight rains occasionally.

[1] See for map the Parliamentary Report on the Mombasa-Victoria Railway, 1898—Africa no. 8.

In working out some of the more obscure Moths, Sir George Hampson has kindly assisted me, both by the loan of pamphlets and by personal examination of structural characters.

The following is a list of the species obtained:—

## I. RHOPALOCERA.

### N Y M P H A L I D Æ.

1. AMAURIS DOMINICANUS.

*Amauris dominicanus*, Trimen, Trans. Ent. Soc. 1879, p. 323.

Mgana. 4th July, 13th and 30th August, 1896; Mombasa, January 1897.

2. AMAURIS OCHLEA.

*Euplœa ochlea*, Boisduval, App. Voy. de Deleg. dans l'Afr. Austr. p. 589 (1847).

Mombasa, 26th April, 1896.

Rather an unusually large female.

3. LIMNAS CHRYSIPPUS, VAR. KLUGI.

*Limnas klugii*, Butler, P. Z. S. 1885, p. 758.

♀, Samburu, British E. Africa, 15th November; ♂ ♀, Taru, Taru Desert, 13th, 16th, 18th, and 20th December, 1896; ♂, Voi, 1st May, 1897.

The specimen from Voi is about one-third larger than any of the others, and one of the specimens obtained on the 20th December is a transitional form towards var. *dorippus*, Klug.

4. MYCALESIS SAFITZA.

*Mycalesis safitza*, Hewitson, Gen. Diurn. Lep. p. 394, pl. 66. fig. 3 (1851).

♂ ♂, Chanjamwe, 28th July; ♂ ♂ ♀, Mgana, 28th August; ♂ ♀, Taru, 16th and 20th December, 1896; ♀, Mombasa, 7th January, 1897.

4 *a*. MYCALESIS EVENUS.

*Mycalesis evenus*, Hopffer, Monatsber. königl. Akad. Wiss. Berl. 1855, p. 641; Peters's Reise n. Mossamb. p. 394, pl. 25. figs. 5, 6 (1862).

*Wet form.* Mgana, 12th July, 1896.

*Dry form* (=*caffra*, Wallgr.). Taru, 19th December, 1896.

Mr. Trimen regards this as a variation of the preceding species, and I think it probable that he is right.

5. SAMANTA PERSPICUA.

*Mycalesis perspicua*, Trimen, Trans. Ent. Soc. Lond. 1873, p. 104, pl. 1. fig. 3 (♂).

♂ ♀, Chanjamwe, 28th July; ♂, Mgana, 28th August, 1896.

### 6. PHYSCÆNURA LEDA.

*Periplysia leda*, Gerstaecker, in Von der Decken's Reisen in Ost-Afrika, iii. 2, p. 371, pl. xv. figs. 3, 3a (1873).

Mgana, 6th, 13th, and 28th August, 1896 ; Maungu Inkubwa, 21st March, 1897.

### 7. MELANITIS SOLANDRA.

*Papilio solandra*, Fabricius, Syst. Ent. p. 500 (1775).

Dry-season ♀, Mgana, 6th August, 1896.

### 8. CHARAXES NEANTHES.

*Nymphalis neanthes*, Hewitson, Exot. Butt. i. p. 88, pl. 44. figs. 2, 3 (1854).

♀, Maungu Inkubwa, 21st March, 1897.

### 9. CHARAXES ZOOLINA.

♀. *Nymphalis zoolina*, Westwood and Hewitson, Gen. Diurn. Lep. pl. liii. fig. 1 (1850).

♂ ♂, Taru, 13th December, 1896 ; Maungu Inkubwa, 21st March, 1897.

### 10. CHARAXES CITHÆRON.

*Charaxes cithæron*, Felder, Wien. ent. Monatschr. iii. p. 398, pl. 8. figs. 2, 3 (1859).

♂ ♂, Maungu Inkubwa, 21st March, 1897.

### 11. CHARAXES VARANES.

*Papilio varanes*, Cramer, Pap. Exot. ii. pl. clx. D, E (1779).

♂ ♂, Maungu Inkubwa, 21st March, 1897.

### 12. JUNONIA LIMNORIA, var. TAVETA.

*Precis taveta*, Rogenhofer, Ann. Hof-Museum, Wien, vi. p. 460, pl. xv. fig. 7 (1891).

♂, Maungu Inkubwa, 21st March, 1897; ♀ ,Taru, 11th December, 1896.

A perfect pair of this species, of which we previously had a poor series.

### 13. JUNONIA GURUANA.

*Precis guruana*, Rogenhofer, Verh. zool.-bot. Gesellsch. Wien, xli. p. 564 (1891).

♂ ♀, Maungu Inkubwa, 21st March, 1897.

A nearly perfect pair of this rare butterfly. Looking at the variability of the allied *J. pelasgis*, it seems possible that this may be an extreme form of the preceding species.

### 14. JUNONIA AURORINA.

*Junonia aurorina*, Butler, P. Z. S. 1893, p. 651, pl. lx. fig. 3.

♂ ♂ ♀ ♀, Maungu Inkubwa, 21st March, 1897.

One very shattered male nearly approaches *J. pyriformis* in colouring, and shows the intensely dry character of that insect on the under surface. It will be remembered that in 1896 (P. Z. S. p. 111) I suggested the possibility of the latter being a form of *J. aurorina.* As the fact that the latter and *J. tugela* fly together in the wet-season in S. Africa seems to disprove the statement that they are seasonal forms of one species, it would appear more probable that *J. pyriformis* is the dry form of *J. aurorina,* the single example of the former in this collection having evidently been a considerable time on the wing; however, we need more evidence before deciding this point, especially as all three of these species have dry-season undersides to the wings.

### 15. JUNONIA CUAMA.

*Junonia cuama,* Hewitson, Exot. Butt. iii., *Jun.* pl. i. figs. 4, 5 (1864).

♀, Maungu Inkubwa, 21st March, 1897.

### 16. JUNONIA CEBRENE.

*Junonia cebrene,* Trimen, Trans. Ent. Soc. Lond. 1870, p. 353.

♂, Samburu, 19th November; ♀ ♀, Taru, 16th December, 1896; ♂ ♀, Maungu Inkubwa, 21st March, 1897.

### 17. JUNONIA CLELIA.

*Papilio clelia,* Cramer, Pap. Exot. i. pl. xxi. E, F (1775).

♂, Mombasa, 4th January, 1897.

### 18. JUNONIA NATALICA.

*Precis natalica,* Felder, Wien. ent. Monatschr. iv. p. 106 (1860).

Taru, 16th December, 1896.

### 19. PROTOGONIOMORPHA NEBULOSA.

*Salamis nebulosa,* Trimen, Trans. Ent. Soc. Lond. 1881, p. 441.

♂ ♀, Mgana, B. E. Africa, 13th and 28th August, 1896.

This is the Eastern form of *P. aglatonice,* from which the male differs very little, the apical black area of the primaries being only slightly broader. I take *P. aglatonice* to be the Western type, the female of which more nearly resembles the male. A third form differing to about the same extent is *P. definita* of Madagascar, which I formerly confounded with males of *P. nebulosa.*

### 20. PYRAMEIS CARDUI.

*Papilio cardui,* Linnæus, Faun. Suec. p. 276 (1761).

Mgana, 2nd September, 1896.

### 21. HYPOLIMNAS MISIPPUS.

*Papilio misippus,* Linnæus, Mus. Lud. Ulr. p. 264 (1764).

♂ ♂, Taru, 16th and 20th December, 1896; Mombasa, January 4th; ♂ ♀ ♀, Maungu Inkubwa, March 21st, 1897.

### 22. EURALIA KIRBYI.

*Euralia kirbyi*, Butler, P. Z. S. 1898, p. 51.

Mgana, 11th August, 1896 (one damaged male).

The sudden appearance in recent collections of this fine species is curious; last year we received two specimens in Mr. Kirby's collection and two from Sir H. Johnston, obtained at Zomba.

### 23. EUXANTHE WAKEFIELDII.

*Godartia wakefieldii*, Ward, Ent. Month. Mag. x. p. 152 (1873); Afr. Lep. pl. 6. fig. 3 (1874).

♂ ♀, Mgana, 2nd and 11th August, 1896.

### 24. HAMANUMIDA DÆDALUS.

*Papilio dædalus*, Fabricius, Syst. Ent. p. 482 (1775).

*Dry form.* ♂, Samburu, 26th October, 1896.

*Wet form.* ♂ ♂ ♀ ♀, Taru. 18th and 19th December, 1896, 17th January, 1897.

### 25. EUPHÆDRA VIOLACEA.

*Euryphene violacea*, Butler, P. Z. S. 1888, p. 91.

♂ ♂, Mombasa, 4th January, and Voi, 1st May, 1897.

Two tolerably good examples of this beautiful species.

### 26. LACHNOPTERA AYRESII.

*Lachnoptera ayresii*, Trimen, Trans. Ent. Soc. Lond. 1879, p. 326; South Afr. Butt. i. pl. iii. figs. 5, 5 *a* (1887).

♀, Maungu Inkubwa, 21st March, 1897.

One very worn example only was obtained.

### 27. ATELLA COLUMBINA.

*Papilio columbina*, Cramer, Pap. Exot. iii. pl. ccxxxviii. A, B, iv. pl. cccxxxvii. D, E (1782).

Chanjamwe, 31st May, 1896; Mombasa, 7th January, 1897.

### 28. NEPTIS AGATHA.

*Papilio agatha*, Cramer, Pap. Exot. iv. pl. cccxxvii. A, B (1782).

Mombasa, 7th January, 1897.

### 29. NEPTIS MARPESSA.

*Neptis marpessa*, Hopffer, Monatsb. königl. Akad. Wiss. Berl. 1855, p. 640; Peters's Reise n. Mossamb., Ins. p. 383, pl. xxiv. figs. 9, 10 (1892).

Maungu Inkubwa, 21st March, 1897.

### 30. EURYTELA FULGURATA.

*Libythea fulgurata*, Boisduval, Faun. Madag. p. 52, pl. 8. fig. 5 (1833).

Mgana, 19th July, 1896.

Only one shattered example was obtained; it does not differ from Malagasy specimens.

### 31. EURYTELA DRYOPE.

*Papilio dryope*, Cramer, Pap. Exot. i. pl. lxxviii. E, F (1779).
Mombasa, 7th January, 1897.

### 32. BYBLIA ILITHYIA.

*Papilio ilithyia*, Drury, Ill. Exot. Ent. ii. pl. 17. figs. 1, 2 (1773).

♂, Mgana, June 22nd ; ♂ ♀, Taru, December 13th and 18th, 1896 ; ♂, Voi, May 2nd, 1897.

The whole of the specimens belong to the typical "wet-season" phase : it must be a long wet season to last from the middle of December to near the end of June !

### 33. PLANEMA MONTANA.

*Planema montana*, Butler, P. Z. S. 1888, p. 91.
*Acræa bertha*, Vuillot, Novit. Lep. xii. pl. xix. fig. 5 (1895).
Maungu Inkubwa, 21st March, 1897.
One good male of this rare species.

### 34. ACRÆA METAPROTEA, var. JACKSONI.

♀. *Planema jacksoni*, E. M. Sharpe, Ann. & Mag. Nat. Hist. ser. 6, vol. v. p. 335 ; Waterhouse, Aid Ident. Ins. pl. clxxxix. fig. 1 (1890).

♂, Maungu Inkubwa, 21st March, 1897.

In males of this Eastern variety the subapical band of primaries is separated by a long interval from the internal patch, as in the Western varieties of the species.

### 35. ACRÆA SERENA, var. PERRUPTA.

*Telchinia perrupta*, Butler, Ann. & Mag. Nat. Hist. ser. 5, vol. xii. p. 102 (1883).

♂ ♀, Mombasa, 4th and 7th January, 1897.

This variation is barely separable from *A. serena*, var. *buxtoni* ; but the male of the latter is usually more brightly coloured, with blacker borders and the black lunate patch closing the cell of the primaries never tending to join the outer borders by means of an intermediate spot : the females of both are extremely variable.

### 36. ACRÆA LYCIA and vars.

*Papilio lycia*, Fabricius, Syst. Ent. p. 464 (1775).
Voi, April 15th and May 1st, 1897.

Var. SGANZINI, Boisduval.
Voi, April 15th and May 2nd, 1897.

Var. DAIRA, Godman.
Voi, April 15th and May 1st and 2nd, 1897.

Not only is there one perfectly intermediate specimen between the variety *A. sganzini* and typical *A. lycia*, but a male of the variety *A. syanzini* was taken on May 2nd *in copulâ* with the variety *A. daira*.

37. ACRÆA CÆCILIA, var. STENOBEA.

*Acræa stenobea*, Wallengren, Wien. ent. Monatschr. iv. p. 35 (1860).

♀, Taru, 18th December, 1896.

This specimen much interests me ; it is the first example of this variety which I have seen from Eastern Africa, has the colouring of the male, but with all the black spots of typical *A. cæcilia* ; it thus fully confirms the correctness of my decision in sinking *A. stenobea* as a mere variety (or, possibly, seasonal form) of *A. cæcilia*.

38. ACRÆA NATALICA.

*Acræa natalica*, Boisduval, App. Voy. de Deleg. p. 590 (1847).

♂ ♀, Mayera, 20th July ; ♀, Mgana, 26th July, 1896.

39. ACRÆA BRÆSIA.

*Acræa bræsia*, Godman, P. Z. S. 1885, p. 538.

Voi, 1st and 2nd May, 1897.

40. ACRÆA CHILO.

*Acræa chilo*, Godman & Salvin, P. Z. S. 1880, p. 184, pl. xix. figs. 4, 5.

♂, Maziwa-Mitatu, 24th March ; Voi, 1st and 2nd May, 1897.

One of the characteristics of typical *A. chilo* is the strongly concave outer margin to its primaries, but in Mr. Betton's series every gradation exists to a distinctly convex outer margin.

41. ACRÆA ANEMOSA.

*Acræa anemosa*, Hewitson, Exot. Butt. iii. pl. 8. figs. 14, 15 (1865).

♀, Samburu, 15th November, 1896 ; ♂, Voi, 1st May, 1897.

42. ACRÆA NEOBULE.

*Acræa neobule*, Doubleday & Hewitson, Gen. Diurn. Lep. pl. xix. fig. 3 (1848).

♀, Mauungu Inkubwa, 21st March ; ♂, Ndara Hills, 6th April, 1897.

43. ACRÆA CRYSTALLINA.

♂. *Acræa crystallina*, H. Grose-Smith, Ann. & Mag. Nat. Hist. ser. 6, vol. v. p. 167 (1890) ; Rhop. Exot. i., *Acræa*, pl. iii. figs. 3, 4 (1892).

♀ ♀, Voi, 1st and 2nd May, 1897.

This species is entirely new to the Museum collection.

44. PARDOPSIS PUNCTATISSIMA.

*Acræa punctatissima*, Boisduval, Faune Ent. Madag. p. 31, pl. 6. fig. 2 (1833).

Mgana, 30th August, 1896.

## LYCÆNIDÆ.

### 45. ALÆNA PICATA.

*Alæna picata*, E. M. Sharpe, Ann. & Mag. Nat. Hist. ser. 6, vol. xvii. p. 126 (1896).

♂, Voi?, B. E. Africa[1].

No exact habitat accompanied the single example of this rare species ; it is quite new to the Museum collection.

### 46. PARAPONTIA SUBPUNCTATA.

*Teriomima subpunctata*, Kirby, Ann. & Mag. Nat. Hist. ser. 5, vol. xix. p. 364 (1887); Grose-Smith & Kirby, Rhop. Exot. i., *Afric. Lyc.* pl. iii. figs. 11, 12 (1888).

♂ ♂, Taru, 16th December, 1896.

Only two males of this rare species were obtained ; it is quite new to the Museum collection. It is now evident that this is an Eastern (not Western) species, and an examination of its neuration and other structural characters, as well as a comparison of the markings of the under surface, make it evident that it is nearly related to *Parapontia undularis*. Mr. Betton's specimens are slightly larger and more distinctly washed with buff on the costal and apical areas of the primaries and the secondaries upon the under surface than in the type.

### 47. TINGRA AMENAIDA.

*Pentila amenaida*, Hewitson, Exot. Butt. v., *Pent. & Lipt.* pl. 2. figs. 4–7 (1873).

Mgana, 13th August ; Taru, 13th, 18th, and 19th December, 1896.

This species is exceedingly variable on both surfaces ; the black border of the primaries above is sometimes reduced to an apical patch, that of the secondaries being reduced to a row of spots or wholly absent, whilst on the under surface the submarginal row of spots is either faintly indicated or entirely wanting. If only single examples of the extreme types were received, they would be unhesitatingly described as distinct species : I have no doubt that *T. nero* and *T. bertha* are varieties, for we have exactly similar specimens, but with smaller spots, whilst the size of the spots is unquestionably extremely variable.

### 48. DURBANIA HILDEGARDA.

*Teriomima?* *hildegarda*, Kirby, Ann. & Mag. Nat. Hist. ser. 5, vol. xix. p. 357 (1887); Grose-Smith & Kirby, Rhop. Exot. i., *Afric. Lyc.* pl. iv. figs. 7, 8 (1888).

Var. *Teriomima freya*, Grose-Smith & Kirby, Rhop. Exot. ii., *Afric. Lyc.* pl. xxv. figs. 1, 2 (1894).

Mgana, 27th June and 13th July ; Samburu, 10th November ;

---

[1] It was amongst a number of Lepidoptera obtained at Voi ; it therefore probably came from that locality.

Taru, 16th, 19th, and 20th December, 1896; Mombasa, 7th January, 1897.

The variation of the markings of the upper surface in this species is considerable and may be thus described:—

1.—*Primaries.* Costal markings not entering the discoidal cell, but forming a **K**-shaped marking immediately beyond cell; outer border wide on costa, rapidly tapering and becoming linear after second median branch, not reaching external angle.

*Secondaries.* Outer border extremely narrow. Mgana.

2.—*Primaries.* Costal markings extending quite across discoidal cell and completely confluent with outer border, which tapers gradually to external angle and extends a short distance along the inner margin. In this variety the outer border occupies about a third of the wing.

*Secondaries.* Outer border broad in the centre, squamose at both extremities. One shattered and worn starved example. Mgana.

3.—*Primaries.* Costal markings extending across discoidal cell, but separated from outer border, which is slightly narrower than in var. 1, but continued to inner margin.

*Secondaries.* With tolerably broad outer border of nearly uniform width (typical *D. hildegarda*). Samburu.

4.—*Primaries.* Costal markings as in var. 1, but outer border continued to inner margin.

*Secondaries.* Outer border distinctly narrower than in var. 3, and especially towards anal angle. Taru.

5.—Like var. 3, excepting that the outer borders of all the wings are broader (typical *D. freya*). Taru.

It is difficult to find two specimens which exactly agree in pattern.

### 49. POLYOMMATUS BÆTICUS.

*Papilio bæticus,* Linnæus, Syst. Nat. i. 2, p. 789 (1767).

♂, Taru, 18th December, 1896.

### 50. CATOCHRYSOPS OSIRIS.

*Lycæna osiris,* Hopffer, Ber. Verh. Ak. Berlin, 1855, p. 642; Peters's Reise n. Mossamb. v. p. 409, pl. 26. figs. 11, 12 (1862).

♀, Mgana, 30th August, 1896; ♂, Maungu Inkubwa, 21st March, 1897.

Only one unusually large pair was obtained.

### 51. CATOCHRYSOPS PERPULCHRA.

*Lycæna perpulchra,* Holland, Entomologist, 1892, Suppl. p. 90; Proc. U.S. Nat. Mus. vol. xviii. p. 239, pl. vii. fig. 7 (1895).

♀, Mombasa, 7th January, 1897.

This is an unusually white example; we possess a similar, though more worn, example from Zomba. My original type of *C. hypoleucus* from the Victoria Nyanza appears to be a distinct species; it is considerably larger, the under surface tinted with buff, all the black spots larger : two additional spots to the discal series of primaries, the lower half of the submarginal stripe of primaries blackish, and that of the secondaries commencing with two short black bars placed angle to angle ; a few black scales are also sprinkled on the other divisions of this stripe.

### 52. CATOCHRYSOPS HIPPOCRATES.

*Papilio hippocrates*, Fabricius, Ent. Syst. iii. p. 288 (1793).

♀, Mgana, 13th August, 1896.

### 53. CUPIDOPSIS JOBATES.

*Lycæna jobates*, Hopffer, Ber. Verh. Ak. Berlin, 1855, p. 642 ; Peters's Reise n. Mossamb. v. p. 408, pl. 26. figs. 9, 10 (1862).

Mgana, 30th August, 1896 ; Mombasa, 4th January, 1897.

### 54. AZANUS JESOUS.

*Polyommatus jesous*, Guérin, Lefebvre's Voy. Abyss. vi. p. 383, pl. 11. figs. 3, 4 (1847).

♀, Mgana, 28th June, 1896 ; ♂ ♂, Voi, 1st May, 1897.

### 55. TARUCUS PLINIUS.

*Hesperia plinius*, Fabricius, Ent. Syst. iii. 1, p. 284 (1793).

♀ ♀, Taru, 22nd November and 20th December, 1896.

### 56. NACADUBA SICHELA.

*Lycæna sichela*, Wallengren, Kongl. Svenska Vetens.-Akad. Handl. 1857 ; Lep. Rhop. Caffr. p. 37.

♂, Voi, 1st May, 1897.

### 57. ZIZERA GAIKA.

*Lycæna gaika*, Trimen, Trans. Ent. Soc. Lond. ser. 3, vol. i. p. 403 (1862).

Mgana, 13th August and " 20th December (N. P. D.)," 1896. N. P. D. are probably the initials of the captor, as Mr. Betton, at the time, was at Taru.

### 58. CASTALIUS MELÆNA, var.

*Lycæna melæna*, Trimen, South-Afr. Butt. ii. p. 82.

Voi, 1st May, 1897.

An extraordinay specimen of what I take to be a very melanistic form of this species, in which the spots on the primaries above are greatly reduced in size and the white area of the secondaries is only represented by an irregular central band : on the under surface the markings are slightly thicker and blacker, but otherwise are identical with those in South-African specimens. We are so badly off for this species that it is possible that similar varieties of the species may occur also in Natal. Until I compared the under-surface pattern in the two insects, I imagined that they would prove to be quite distinct.

### 59. Lycæna kersteni.

*Lycæna kersteni*, Gerstaecker, in Von der Decken's Reisen in Ost-Afrika, iii. 2, p. 373, pl. xv. fig. 5 (1873).

♂ ♂, Taru, 20th December, 1896 ; Voi, 1st May, 1897.
This is the Eastern representative of *L. larydas*; it has much more white on the under surface.

### 60. Lycænesthes sylvanus.

*Papilio sylvanus*, Drury, Ill. Exot. Ent. ii. pl. iii. figs. 2, 3 (1773).

♂ ♂, Mgana, 13th August, 1896.
These are the first examples from Eastern Africa which I have hitherto seen; unfortunately only one pair was obtained.

### 61. Lycænesthes amarah.

*Polyommatus amarah*, Guérin in Lefebvre's Voy. Abyss. vi. p. 384, pl. 11. figs. 5, 6 (1847).

♂, Mgana, 12th July, 1896.

### 62. Zeritis amanga.

*Zeritis amanga*, Westwood in Oates's Matabele-land, p. 351 (1881).

♀, Taru, 20th December, 1896 ; ♂, Voi, 2nd May, 1897.
The specimen of the female differs from our single imperfect Abyssinian example in the pattern of the primaries ; the male, however, undoubtedly varies not a little.

### 63. Zeritis harpax.

*Papilio harpax*, Fabricius, Syst. Ent., App. p. 829 (1775).

♂ ♀, Mwachi River, June 7th ; ♀, Mgana, August 30th, 1896.
Var. ? ♂ with red patch on primaries confined to internal area ; secondaries of both sexes slightly less heavily bordered ; silver spotting on under surface of secondaries considerably less prominent and (in the female) on a paler background.
♂ ♀, Mgana, 12th July, 1896.
It is just barely possible that the variety noted above may be distinct from typical *Z. harpax*, but I do not believe it is so ; we have received the same form from Nyasaland. I also do not believe it possible to separate *Z. perion* from *Z. harpax*, the differences given to distinguish them by Mr. Trimen being undoubtedly unreliable.

### Leptomyrina, gen. nov.

Nearly related to typical *Myrina* (*M. silenus*, &c.), having the same general wing outline and neuration ; it differs in its comparatively longer and far more slender antennæ with abruptly thickened club, rather more slender palpi, and the considerably shorter and more delicate tails to the secondaries. Type *L. phidias*, Fabr. (*rabe*, Boisd.).

64. LEPTOMYRINA HIRUNDO.

*Thecla hirundo,* Wallengren, Kongl. Svenska Vetensk.-Akad. Handl. 1857, p. 35 (*Amblypodia h.*); Trimen, Rhop. Afr. Austr. ii. p. 230, pl. 4. fig. 11 (1866).

Maungu Inkubwa, 21st March, 1897.

This is the most southern example of *L. hirundo* that I have heard of; our two examples are both from Natal.

65. VIRACHOLA LIVIA?

*Lycæna livia,* Klug, Symb. Phys. pl. 40. figs. 3–6 (1834).

♂, Mgana, 12th July, 1896.

The male is somewhat shattered, but differs remarkably from Arabian examples, all the markings below being bright mahogany-red with blackish margins and whitish borders; the internal area of primaries buff.

66. VIRACHOLA LORISONA, var.

*Myrina lorisona,* Hewitson, Ill. Diurn. Lep. p. 37, pl. 16. figs. 48, 49 (1863).

♂, Mgana, 12th July, 1896.

The single example obtained differs so much from Hewitson's type in the pattern of the upper surface, that, if we had not possessed an intermediate specimen from West Africa, I should have concluded that this Eastern variety must be distinct: the secondaries would be best described as bright orange tawny, the base, abdominal border, and a submedian streak smoky greyish brown; the usual bright blue subcostal sexual spot; outer border narrowly dark brown, slightly widest at apex: the orange patch on the primaries is also much larger than in typical *V. lorisona.* This is the first example which I have seen from East Africa.

67. VIRACHOLA DIOCLES.

*Deudorix diocles,* Hewitson, Ill. Diurn. Lep., Suppl. p. 12, pl. v. figs. 55, 56 (1869).

♂, Mgana, 26th July; ♀, Mayeras, 20th July, 1896.

A single pair of this rare species was obtained; it is new to the general Collection. The female above is smoky greyish-brown, the primaries with a diffused ashy patch between the cell and the submedian vein; the secondaries with a similar patch on the median and lower radial interspaces; the anal lobe is externally golden orange, the usual internal black spot being sprinkled with silvery blue scales: otherwise, excepting in its rounder wings, it much resembles females of *V. livia.*

68. VIRACHOLA DARIAVES.

*Deudorix dariaves,* Hewitson, Ent. Month. Mag. xiii. p. 205 (1877).

♂, Mgana, 23rd July, 1896.

Also new to the general Collection.

69. VIRACHOLA ANTALUS.

*Dipsas antalus*, Hopffer, Monatsb. königl. Akad. Wissensch. Berlin, 1855, p. 641.

*Sithon antalus*, Peters's Reise n. Mossamb., Ins. p. 400, pl. xxv. figs. 7-9 (1862).

♂ ♀, Mgana, 13th August, 1896.

70. IOLAUS PHILIPPUS.

*Hesperia philippus*, Fabricius, Ent. Syst. iii. 1, p. 283 (1793).

♀, Mgana, 13th August; ♂ ♀, Taru, 19th December, 1896; ♂ ♂ ♀ ♀, Mombasa, 7th January, 1897.

71. IOLAUS PACHALICUS.

*Hypolycæna pachalica*, Butler, P. Z. S. 1888, p. 69.

♀, Chanjamwe, British East Africa, 31st May: ♂ ♂, Taru, December 20th, 1896; Mombasa, 7th January, 1897.

72. ARGIOLAUS SILARUS.

*Iolaus silarus*, H. H. Druce, Ent. Month. Mag. vol. xxii. p. 154 (1885).

♂ ♂, Taru, 18th December, 1896, and 1st February, 1897; ♀, Ndara Hills, 7th April, 1897.

This beautiful species, of which unfortunately only three examples were obtained, is quite new to the Museum collection.

PAPILIONIDÆ.

73. MYLOTHRIS AGATHINA.

*Papilio agathina*, Cramer, Pap. Exot. iii. pl. ccxxxvii. D, E (1782).

♂ ♀, Mgana, 2nd & 6th August; Taru, 16th December, 1896.

74. NYCHITONA MEDUSA, var. ALCESTA.

*Papilio alcesta*, Cramer, Pap. Exot. iv. pl. ccclxxix. A (1782).

Mgana, 22nd June, 2nd & 11th August, 1896; Mombasa, 4th January; Maungu Inkubwa, 21st March, 1897.

After arranging the fine combined series of the Museum and Godman and Salvin collections, I have been forced to the conclusion that, at most, the genus *Nychitona* consists of two very variable species—*N. medusa* (African) and *N. xiphia* (Asiatic): but, even then, several of the forms of each species are barely, if at all, distinguishable. In Kirby's Catalogue Cramer's incorrect locality 'Coast of Bengal' is adopted for *N. medusa*; but the insect figured is of a purely African variety and was probably received from Sierra Leone.

75. TERIAS BRIGITTA, var. ZOE.

*Terias zoe*, Hopffer, Ber. Verh. Akad. Berl. 1855, p. 640; Peters's Reise n. Mossamb. v. p. 369, pl. 23. figs. 10, 11 (1862).

♂, Chanjamwe, 28th July, 1896; ♂, Manjewa, 13th January, 1897.

76. TERIAS SENEGALENSIS.

*Terias senegalensis,* Boisduval, Sp. Gén. Lép. i. p. 672 (1836).

♂ ♂ , Taru, 16th & 19th December, 1896.

Var. BISINUATA, Butler, Ann. & Mag. Nat. Hist. ser. 4, vol. xviii. p. 485 (1876).

♀ Samburu, 15th November, 1896.

77. TERACOLUS CALAIS.

*Papilio calais,* Cramer, Pap. Exot. i. pl. liii. C, D (1779).

♂ ♀ , Taru, 13th & 18th December, 1896 ; Voi, 1st May, 1897.

78. TERACOLUS ERIS.

*Pontia eris,* Klug, Symb. Phys., Ins. pl. vi. figs. 15, 16 (1829).

♀ . *Teracolus abyssinicus,* Butler, Ann. & Mag. Nat. Hist. ser. 4, vol. xviii. p. 486 (1876).

*Wet form.* ♂ ♂ ♀ ♀ , Taru, 22nd November, 13th, 16th, 19th, & 20th December, 1896 ; 17th January, 1897.

*Intermediate form.* ♂ ♂ ♀ , Maziwa-ya-Tayau, 16th February, 1897.

The eighteen examples obtained by Mr. Betton show the usual uniformity of pattern characteristic of the Northern species of this group, and are all readily separable from the Southern, East-Central, and Western species, which Mr. Marshall proposed to unite under one name : only one example of the yellow female (to which I gave the name of *T. abyssinicus*) was obtained ; indeed yellow females of the *T. eris* group seem to be rare.

79. TERACOLUS PUNICEUS.

♂ . *Teracolus puniceus,* Butler, P. Z. S. 1888, p. 72 ; ♂ ♀ , 1894, pl. xxxvi. figs. 5, 6.

♂ ♂ , Taru, 16th & 18th December, 1896.

80. TERACOLUS HETÆRA.

♂ . *Callosune hetæra,* Gerstaecker, Arch. für Naturg. 1871, p. 357 ; Von der Decken's Reisen in Ost-Afrika, iv. 2, p. 365, pl. xv. fig. 2 (1873).

♂ ♂ ♀ , Taru, 16th, 18th, & 20th December, 1896.

The wet form of the male and the yellow form of the female of this species are new to the Museum series. Most of the specimens are of wet or intermediate types, but one female combines a wet-season upper surface with an extreme dry form of under surface.

81. TERACOLUS IMPERATOR.

*Teracolus imperator,* Butler, P. Z. S. 1876, p. 132.

♂ ♂ , Mgana, 28th August ; ♀ , Samburu, 15th November ; ♂ ♂ ♀ ♀ , Taru, 18th to 20th December, 1896.

A ♀ whitish-spotted black-tipped form of the wet-season phase as well as a magenta-glossed crimson-tipped example (both new to me) were in the series.

### 82. TERACOLUS BETTONI, sp. n.

♂. *Teracolus phlegyas* (part), Butler, cf. P. Z. S. 1894, p. 574.

This species at all seasons differs from the preceding in the extremely narrow and much more glistening lilac apical patch or band on the primaries of the male, its black inner edging almost or wholly wanting, and in the deep indentation or complete separation of the internal black stripe on the primaries of the female; the latter sex is either white or yellow, the apical area being either crossed by an orange patch or a row of white spots as in *T. imperator*. The dry form of the male differs chiefly from the wet form in the rosy colouring of the apex of the primaries and the whole surface of the secondaries on the under surface, whilst extreme wet types of the male are not only pearly white below, but show an oblique discal series of black spots between the costal vein and second median branch on the underside of the secondaries: the female of the dry phase resembles the wet form of *T. phlegyas* on the upperside and the dry form of that species on the underside; it is, however, larger and shows heavier black markings. Expanse of wings, ♂ 58–71 millim., ♀ 62–69 millim.

*Wet form.* ♂ ♂ ♀ ♀, Taru, 24th & 25th November, 15th, 18th, 19th, & 20th December, 1896 (one pair taken *in copulâ*).

*Intermediate form.* ♂, Mgana, 2nd August, 1896.

Small, and with white unspotted under surface.

*Dry form.* ♀, Ndara Hills, 7th April, 1897.

Fifteen examples were in Mr. Betton's collection.

### 83. TERACOLUS INCRETUS.

*Teracolus incretus*, Butler, Ent. Month. Mag. xviii. p. 146 (1881).

♀ ♀, Mgana, 30th August, and Samburu, 15th November; ♂, Taru, 18th December, 1896.

### 84. TERACOLUS EVARNE.

*Pontia evarne*, Klug, Symb. Phys. pl. vi. figs. 1–4 (1829).

*Wet form.* ♂ ♂, Mombasa, 7th January, 1897.

*Intermediate form.* ♂, Mgana, 27th June, 1896 (= *T. syrtinus*).

*Dry form.* ♂, Voi, 4th July, 1897 (= *T. citreus*).

### 85. TERACOLUS HEUGLINI (vars. T. THRUPPI & JACKSONI).

*Teracolus thruppi*, Butler, P. Z. S. 1885, p. 770, pl. xlvii. fig. 10 (Intermediate form.)

*Teracolus jacksoni*, E. M. Sharpe, Ann. & Mag. Nat. Hist. ser. 6, vol. v. p. 336 (1890). (Wet form.)[1]

---

[1] The two forms seem to occur together at the commencement and end of the wet season, so far as I can judge; but they differ very little. A more marked intermediate form may perhaps exist.

♂ ♀, Mgana, 19th July, 13th & 30th August; ♂, Samburu, 26th October: ♂ ♂ ♀ ♀, Taru, 13th, 18th, & 20th December, 1896.

### 86. TERACOLUS XANTHUS.

*Teracolus xanthus*, Swinhoe, P. Z. S. 1884, p. 440, pl. xxxix. fig. 10.

*Wet form.* ♂ ♂, Taru, 13th & 20th December, 1896; Mombasa, 7th January, 1897.

*Intermediate form.* ♂ ♂, Samburu, 26th October and 6th November, 1896.

### 87. TERACOLUS ANTEVIPPE.

*Anthocharis antevippe*, Boisduval, Sp. Gén. Lép. i. p. 572 (1836).

Extreme wet form (var. *subvenosus*, Butler). ♂ ♂, Mgana, 28th August, 1896; Mombasa, 7th January; Manjewa, 13th January, 1897.

### 88. TERACOLUS GAVISA.

*Anthopsyche gavisa*, Wallengren, Lep. Rhop. Caffr. p. 13 (1857).

♂ ♀, Samburu, 15th November; ♀, Taru, 18th December, 1896.

### 89. TERACOLUS EXOLE.

*Anthocharis exole* ♂, Reiche, Ferr. & Gal. Voy. Abyss. pl. xxxi. fig. 4 (1849).

Intermediate form (var. *roxane*, Felder). ♂ ♀, Taru, 22nd November and 16th December, 1896.

As these were sent in one envelope it is probable that they were taken *in coitu*. This is an argument in favour of the distinctness of *T. exole* from *T. omphale*: the male is imperfect.

### 90. TERACOLUS OMPHALE.

*Pieris omphale*, Godart, Enc. Méth. ix. p. 122 (1819).

*Wet form.* ♂ ♂, Mgana, 13th & 28th August; Samburu, 1st November; ♀, Taru, 13th December, 1896; ♂, Mombasa, 7th January; Maungu Inkubwa, 21st March, 1897.

### 91. TERACOLUS PSEUDACASTE.

*Teracolus pseudacaste*, Butler, P. Z. S. 1876, p. 156, pl. vi. fig. 11.

*Intermediate form.* ♂ ♂, Samburu, 26th & 28th October, 6th November; ♂ ♀, 15th November, 1896.

*Wet form.* ♂ ♂, Taru, 16th December, 1896; Mombasa, 7th January, 1897, ♀ same date.

The female from Mombasa is the blackest and most interesting variety that I have seen.

92. Teracolus leo.

*Teracolus leo*, Butler, Ann. & Mag. Nat. Hist. ser. 3, vol. xvi. p. 397 (1865).

*Wet-season form.* ♀, Taru, 19th December, 1896.

*Dry-season form.* ♀, Mbuyuni, 14th June, 1897; ♂ ♂, Voi, 4th July, 1897.

The dry form is quite new to science (excepting for the single starved and faded male without locality noted in my Revision of the genus, *cf.* Ann. & Mag. Nat. Hist. ser. 6, vol. xx. p. 501, 1897). The male at this season chiefly differs from that of the wet-season in the bluer tint of the grey basal area of the primaries, but the orange is sometimes carried above the first median branch and the dusky submarginal markings are sometimes wanting; the underside differs in its flesh-coloured suffusion, which is very well-defined at apex of primaries and over the basal, costal, and internal areas of the secondaries. The female of the dry form resembles *T. cœlestis* of Swinhoe (the dry form of the female of *T. halimede*), but has the discal black spots across the primaries widely separated from the outer border by a broad intervening belt of the yellow ground-colour: on the underside the apex of the primaries and the whole of the secondaries are fleshy brown, and the transverse spots are much darker than in *T. cœlestis*.

93. Teracolus venosus.

♂. *Idmais venosa*, Staudinger, Exot. Schmett. p. 43, pl. xxiii. (1885); ♀, Holland, Proc. U.S. Nat. Mus. vol. xviii. p. 759 (1896).

♂ ♂ ♀ ♀, Taru, 22nd November; 13th, 16th, 18th, & 19th December, 1896.

This species was badly needed for the Museum series; therefore I was pleased to find that Mr. Betton had secured a fair number of specimens.

94. Teracolus helvolus, var.

*Teracolus helvolus*, Butler, P. Z. S. 1888, p. 94.

♀, Mbuyuni, 7th April; ♂, Voi, 25th April; between Voi and Ndi (88 miles from Mombasa), 16th May; Voi, 4th July, 1897.

These specimens are particularly interesting; they are almost as large as *T. aurigineus*, but of the exact pattern and coloration of the dry form of *T. helvolus*. We have corresponding examples of the wet form obtained at Kilimanjaro; a specimen of the latter from Mombasa, however, scarcely differs in size from Somali examples.

95. Teracolus catachrysops.

*Teracolus catachrysops*, Butler, Ann. & Mag. Nat. Hist. ser. 5, vol. ii. p. 178 (1878).

*Dry form.* ♀, Chanjamwe, 18th June, 1896.

*Wet form.* ♂ ♂ ♀, Mombasa, 4th January, 1897.

I now have another proof of the absurdity of calling this very distinct species a variety of *T. mutans*, inasmuch as the dry form is seen to differ from the wet chiefly in the redder colouring of the bands on the under surface, whereas in *T. mutans* the whole under surface of the secondaries and of the apex of primaries becomes clay-coloured with a pink suffusion, the bands being indistinct.

### 96. TERACOLUS PROTOMEDIA.

*Pontia protomedia*, Klug, Symb. Phys., Ins. pl. viii. figs. 13, 14 (1829).

♂ ♂ ♀, Taru, 20th December, 1896.

### 97. CATOPSILIA FLORELLA.

*Papilio florella*, Fabricius, Syst. Ent. p. 479 (1775).

♂, Chanjamwe, 10th June; ♂ ♀, Taru, 18th & 19th December, 1896; ♂ ♀, Maungu Inkubwa, 21st March; ♂ ♂, Ndara Hills, 6th & 7th April, 1897.

### 98. PHRISSURA LASTI.

*Mylothris lasti*, Grose-Smith, Ann. & Mag. Nat. Hist. ser. 6, vol. iii. p. 124 (1889); Rhop. Exot. ii. *Belen.* pl. ii. figs. 1–3 (1892).

♂, Mgana, 26th July; ♂ ♀, 13th August, 1896.

### 99. BELENOIS THYSA.

*Pieris thysa*, Hopffer, Ber. Verh. Akad. Berl. 1855, p. 639; Peters's Reise n. Mossamb., Ins. p. 349, pl. xxi. figs 7–10 (1862).

♂ ♀, Mgana, 2nd August, 1896.

### 100. BELENOIS CREONA.

*Papilio creona*, Cramer, Pap. Exot. i. pl. xcv. C–F (1779).

♂ ♀, Mgana, 13th July; ♂ ♂, Chanjamwe, 28th July; Taru, 20th December, 1896; and Voi, 1st May, 1897.

### 101. BELENOIS MESENTINA, var. LORDACA.

*Pieris lordaca*, Walker, Entomologist, 1870, p. 48.

♂ ♂ ♀ ♀, Maziwa-ya Tayau, 8th to 17th February, 1897.

Mr. Betton took no less than twenty-eight examples of this abundant species, most of them having been caught on the 16th February.

### 102. BELENOIS GIDICA.

*Pieris gidica*, Godart, Enc. Méth. ix. p. 131 (1819).

♂ ♂, Mgana, 28th June; Taru, 18th & 19th December, 1896; Maungu Inkubwa, 21st March, 1897.

All four specimens (including that obtained at the end of June) are of the wet-season phase.

103. GLUTOPHRISSA CONTRACTA, var.

*Glutophrissa contracta*, Butler, P. Z. S. 1888, p. 75.

*Dry form.* ♂ ♀, Mgana, 12th July, 1896.

A rather shattered pair was obtained, but the specimens are of great interest to us as showing the seasonal modification of the species. The dry form somewhat resembles *G. flavida* of Madagascar (which is doubtless the dry form of *G. malatha*), but it differs in the well-defined outer border on the upperside of the secondaries and in the character of the male, which does not differ from wet-season examples of *G. contracta*.

104. PINACOPTERYX LILIANA.

*Belenois liliana*, Grose-Smith, Ann. & Mag. Nat. Hist. ser. 6, vol. iii. p. 122 (1889); Rhop. Exot. ii. pl. i. figs. 7-9 (1893).

♂. Mgana, 22nd June; ♀, Samburu, 15th November, 1896.

105. HERPÆNIA MELANARGE.

*Herpænia melanarge*, Butler, P. Z. S. 1885, p. 774.
*Herpænia iterata*, Butler, P. Z. S. 1888, p. 96.

Dry-season form (*H. melanarge*). ♂, Mgana, 26th July, 1896.

Wet-season form (*H. iterata*). ♀, Taru, 22nd November, ♂ 16th December, ♀ 19th December, 1896.

106. LEUCERONIA BUQUETII.

*Callidryas buquetii*, Boisduval, Sp. Gén. Lép. i. p. 607 (1836).

Taru, 13th, 19th, & 20th December, 1896; Voi, 1st May, 1897.

107. ERONIA DILATATA.

*Eronia dilatata*, Butler, P. Z. S. 1888, p. 96.

Mgana, 6th, 11th, & 30th August; Samburu, 26th October; Taru, 22nd November, 13th & 16th December, 1896; Maungu Inkubwa, 21st March, 1897.

The dry form has slightly narrower black borders to the wings and a slightly deeper-coloured underside than the wet form.

108. ERONIA LEDA.

*Dryas leda*, Boisduval, App. Voy. de Deleg. p. 588 (1847).

♂ ♂ ♀, Maungu Inkubwa, 21st March, 1897.

109. PAPILIO CORINNEUS.

*Papilio corinneus*, Bertoloni, Mem. Acc. Bologna, 1849, p. 9, pl. i. figs. 1-4.

Chanjamwe, 14th June, 1896; Mombasa, 4th January, 1897.

110. PAPILIO PHILONOE.

*Papilio philonoe*, Ward, Ent. Month. Mag. x. p. 152 (1873).

Mombasa, 7th January; Maungu Inkubwa, 21st March, 1897.

### 111. PAPILIO DEMOLEUS.

*Papilio demoleus*, Linnæus, Mus. Lud. Ulr. p. 214 (1764).

Taru, 18th & 20th December, 1896; Mombasa, 4th January; Maungu Inkubwa, 21st March; between Voi and Ndi, 19th May, 1897.

### 112. PAPILIO CONSTANTINUS.

*Papilio constantinus*, Ward, Ent. Month. Mag. viii. p. 34 (1871); Afric. Lep. i. pl. i. figs. 1, 2 (1873).

Two pairs, Maungu Inkubwa, 21st March, 1897.

### 113. PAPILIO NIREUS.

*Papilio nireus*, Linnæus, Mus. Lud. Ulr. p. 217 (1764).

♀, Mombasa, 4th January; ♂ ♂ ♀, Maungu Inkubwa, 21st March, 1897.

I must confess that I see no possible reason for separating this variable species under two distinctive names.

### 114. PAPILIO MEROPE (var. DARDANUS, Brown).

*Papilio merope*, Cramer, Pap. Exot. ii. pl. cli. A, B (1779).

♂ ♂ ♀, Maungu Inkubwa, 21st March, 1897.

Although I do not consider that the Eastern type should be regarded as identical with the Western, it is more convenient (until the forms of so-called *P. merope* have been thoroughly studied) to retain this name for them all. The Southern form is apparently identical with the Eastern one, but the true *P. merope* of Cramer seems to me to be the West-African type with black-and-white female. The corresponding Eastern form is that now received, the female being also of the black-and-white type, but the male differing in constantly having a broad continuous black belt across the secondaries; it thus comes nearest to the male of *P. cenea*, which Mr. Trimen regards as a variety of the same species: perhaps he has proved this point, but it seems odd for the same insect to mimic two totally dissimilar *Danainæ*.

## HESPERIIDÆ.

### 115. SARANGESA ELIMINATA.

*Sarangesa eliminata*, Holland, P. Z. S. 1896, p. 9, pl. v. fig. 2.

Taru, 22nd November and 20th December, 1896; Voi, 22nd April, 2nd May, and 22nd June, 1897.

The specimen obtained on the 22nd April is a distinct intergrade to *S. pertusa*, and I believe, when the species of this group are better understood, it will be found impossible to separate most of the species of the *S. motozi* group; they are simply ridiculously close, whilst (so far as I can judge from our poor series) they probably all occur together. We have *S. pertusa*, *S. synestalmenus*, and *S. motozioides* occurring with *S. motozi* in Nyasaland; *S. per-*

*usa* and *S. motozi* in South Africa ; *S. pertusa* var. and *S. eliminata* in British East Africa at the same spot ; we have *S. pertusa* from Aden, and *S. eliminata* from Abyssinia. Altogether these forms do not look like good distinct species.

116. SARANGESA DJÆLÆLÆ.

*Pterygospidea djælælæ*, Wallengren, Kongl. Svensk. Vetensk.-Akad. Handl. 1857 ; Lep. Rhop. Caffr. p. 54.

Maungu Inkubwa, 21st March, 1897.

117. PYRGUS BETTONI, sp. n. (Plate XXXII. fig. 1.)

Nearest to *P. zebra* and *P. asterodia*, but not very closely allied to any African species known to me, and on the upper surface somewhat resembling the New-World *P. asychis*. Upper surface black-brown ; a white spot near the base of each discoidal cell ; a central interrupted white belt, not reaching the borders of the wings, commencing with a subcostal dot on the primaries, where it is divided into three quadrate spots by the first and second median branches, oblique and terminating in a subconfluent dot on the secondaries ; a transverse trifid subapical white bar on the primaries, and a single small spot on the second median interspace ; submarginal series of dots unequal, the first, second, and fifth extremely minute ; in the secondaries the first, fourth, fifth, and sixth extremely minute ; fringe white, varied with blackish at the extremities of the veins : body normal. Primaries below dark greyish, but with the usual copper-brown reflections ; white spots broader and more confluent than above, internal border greyish white ; secondaries with the basal two-thirds and abdominal border white ; a spot across the base of the cell and a broad irregular oblique belt from near base of costa across the cell, a short central costal streak and a spot just below the latter, greyish olivaceous ; external third occupied by a broad belt of the same colour, slightly flecked with whitish and grey at apex and towards anal angle (so as vaguely to indicate the pale outer border which occurs in *P. zebra*); fringe of all the wings white, spotted with grey. Body below sordid white, the venter rather purer than the pectus. Expanse of wings 24 millim.

Maungu Inkubwa, 21st March, 1897.

118. PYRGUS DROMUS.

*Pyrgus dromus*, Plötz, Mitth. naturw. Vereins, 1884, p. 6.

Mgana, 30th August, 1896.

Unfortunately only a single example of this pretty little *Pyrgus* was obtained.

119. PAROSMODES ICTERIA.

*Pamphila icteria*, Mabille, C.R. Soc. Ent. Belg. vol. xxxv. p. clxxx (1821).

Mgana, 5th July, 13th & 30th August, 1896.

28*

### 120. BAORIS FATUELLUS.

*Pamphila fatuellus*, Hopffer, Monatsber. k. Akad. Wissensch. Berl. 1855, p. 643; Peters's Reise n. Mossamb., Ins. p. 417, pl. xxvii. figs. 3, 4 (1862).

Mwachi River, 7th June, 1896.

### 121. BAORIS AURITINCTUS, sp. n.    (Plate XXXII. fig. 2.)

Form of *B. fatuellus*, primaries with exactly similar transparent white spots; an elliptical patch below the median vein and the commencement of its first branch, a small spot above the submedian vein (representing the white spot frequently present in *B. fatuellus*), and a pilose internal streak bronzy ochraceous, the whole wing-surface also glossed with golden bronze: secondaries more distinctly glossed with golden, the long hair clothing the discoidal and internal areas to the centre of the disc being bronzy ochraceous ; two unequal subapical transparent yellowish spots placed obliquely; fringes of all the wings smoky brown, tipped with bone-white excepting towards apex of primaries.  Body of the ordinary type, blackish with bronzy green reflections on head and thorax and golden cupreous reflections on abdomen; a shoulder-spot and a spot on each side of the head, close to the eyes, ochreous ; antennæ bronze tipped with purplish black.  Under surface brownish grey, densely irrorated with ochraceous excepting on the internal areas : otherwise very like *B. fatuellus*.  Expanse of wings 34 millim.

Taru, 20th December, 1896.

Only one example obtained.

### 122. CERATRICHIA STELLATA.

*Ceratrichia stellata*, Mabille, C.R. Soc. Ent. Belg. 1891, p. lxv.

Mgana, 13th & 28th August, 1896.

I quite agree with Dr. Holland that this species differs from typical *Ceratrichia* in its shorter antennæ, &c., but I do not like it a bit better in *Cyclopides* (which it is not half so much like in pattern). As Dr. Holland has not proposed a new generic location for it, I prefer, for the present, to let the species rest where M. Mabille placed it.

### 123. RHOPALOCAMPTA FORESTAN.

*Papilio forestan*, Cramer, Pap. Exot. iv. pl. cccxci. E, F (1782).

Ndara Hills, 7th April, 1897.

The Moths in the collection are not in such good condition as the Butterflies, but most of them are recognizable ; some are of great beauty and quite new to the Museum collection ; others we had previously only received from South Africa or from the West coast.  As might be expected, not a few are new to science. The following is as complete an account of them as could be made.

## II. HETEROCERA.

### SYNTOMIDÆ.

#### 124. APISA CANESCENS.

*Apisa canescens*, Walker, Lep. Het. iv. p. 917 (1855).

Camp near 119 miles inland from Mombasa, 7th July, 1897.

The single female example is smaller than any example of that sex which I have hitherto seen, but we have no East-African speci- mens obtained further north than Natal. It is just possible that this may be a small race of the species, as Sir George Hampson informs me that he has seen a male from East Africa still smaller than the female now received.

#### 125. EUCHROMIA AMŒNA.

*Euchromia amœna*, Moeschler, Stett. ent. Zeit. xxxiii. p. 350 (1872).

Mayera, 17th July ; Taru, 20th December, 1896.

This is the species which I called *E. africana* ; Herr Moeschler erroneously gave Silhet as its habitat.

### ARCTIIDÆ.

#### 126. ALOA BIVITTATA, sp. n.   (Plate XXXII. fig. 3.)

Most nearly allied to *A. punctistriga* from India. Primaries cream-coloured, the costal border and veins pale testaceous ; a black dot at base of submedian veins, and a black dot on the lower discocellular vein pierced by a longitudinal blackish-brown streak which runs to outer margin ; a second short and more slender streak, in the areole above it, also running to outer margin ; secondaries pure white. Antennæ white with black pectinations ; head ochreous, becoming chalky white at sides and back of collar ; thorax chalky white ; abdomen ochreous, white at base and with dorsal transverse black bars, of which the first and seventh are widest and the fourth to sixth most delicate ; a black spot on each side of anal segment. Wings below white, the primaries with buff costal borders ; pectus white, smoky brown in front ; legs smoky brown, the hind femora pale ochreous in front ; venter white, with a blackish lateral stripe not extending over the last two segments. Expanse of wings 41 millim.

Mbana, 28th June, 1896.

Only one example was obtained.

#### 127. LACYDES ARBORIFERA.

*Lacydes arborifera*, Butler, Cist. Ent. ii. p. 26 (1875).

Samburu, 1st November, 1896.

Previously only recorded from West Africa.

#### 128. LACYDES GRACILIS, sp. n.   (Plate XXXII. fig. 4.)

♀ . Allied to *L. vocula* and *L. smithii* (*Conchylia smithii*, Holland) :

primaries comparatively narrower [1], pale cupreous brown; a silvery white costal streak from base tapering to a point just before the basal third; the remainder of costal area unmarked almost to apex, where a silvery white band commences, runs obliquely to the upper radial (vein 6), where it joins a longitudinal discoidal streak tapered at each extremity and commencing in the cell just beyond the termination of the costal streak; a longitudinal interno-median streak tapering towards the base and confluent on outer margin, with a short narrower stripe above the first median branch, thus forming a kind of L-shaped character; above the latter along the outer border is a cuneiform patch of silvery white, deeply incised at third median branch; base of internal border white, terminated by an oblique spot of brown slightly darker than the ground-colour, beyond which is a whitish patch; secondaries pearly white, unspotted. Body much rubbed, but probably very similar to that of *L. vocula*. Under surface of wings as above, excepting that the ground-colour of the primaries is a little paler and greyer. Expanse of wings 35 millim.

Marago ya Fundi, Taru desert, 2nd March, 1897.

Unfortunately only one example was obtained, but it seems to differ too much from either of the species above noted to be a variety; the absence of the white costal markings and the much more regular character of the markings seem likely to be trustworthy distinctions.

I am quite unable to identify the following with any genus of *Lithosiinæ* :—

### BETTONIA, gen. nov.

Nearest to *Dictenus* (Butl.), general aspect of *Eubaphe*; the palpi extremely small, slender, directed forwards; proboscis short but well-developed; antennæ (of female) about one-third the length of primaries, simple, somewhat thick; primaries elongate-triangular, costal vein running to second third of costa; subcostal five-branched, the second and third from a long footstalk, the fourth and fifth from a short footstalk; secondaries with the subcostal branches from a long footstalk; the other veins all well separated at their origins. Type *B. ferruginea*.

### 129. BETTONIA FERRUGINEA, sp. n. (Plate XXXII. fig. 5.)

♀. Tawny ferruginous; primaries above with a slightly greyish tinge and a black spot in the centre of the discoidal cell; all the wings with a black discocellular spot. Expanse of wings 20 millim.

♀, Voi, 2nd May, 1897.

### 130. LEXIS BIPUNCTIGERA.

*Lithosia bipunctigera*, Wallengren, Wien. ent. Monatschr. 1860, p 45.

---

[1] This is, however, probably only a sexual character.

*Lexis bipunctigera*, Wallengren, *l. c.* 1863, p. 146.
*Setina quadrinotata*, Walker, Cat. Lep. Het. xxxi. p. 237 (1864).
♀, Maungu Inkubwa, 21st March, 1897.

Of this species we only possess Walker's rather imperfect type from Natal; it is, therefore, a welcome addition.

The genus *Lexis* is allied to *Sozuza*, although the pattern of *L. bipunctigera* ♀ reminds one rather forcibly of that of *Œonistis quadra* ♀ (to which it is certainly not closely related). It is characterized as distinct from *Sozuza* by the absence of the post-discoidal areole (or false cell) in the primaries, by the much greater length of the costal vein, with which the first subcostal branch anastomoses; the third and fourth branches emitted as in *Sozuza*, but the fifth branch emitted from the fourth instead of from before the emission of the third. In the secondaries the so-called second and third median branches (now recognized as the second median and lower radial) form a much shorter furca than in *Sozuza*.

### NYCTEMERIDÆ.

#### 131. TERINA TENUIS.

*Aletis tenuis*, Butler, P. Z. S. 1878, p. 385.
*Terina fulva*, Hampson, Ann. & Mag. Nat. Hist. ser. 6, vol. vi. p. 183 (1891).

Mgana, 13th August, 1896.

A beautiful species of which we should have been glad to obtain examples; unfortunately Mr. Betton only secured one.

#### 132. PITTHEA TRIFASCIATA.

*Türckheimia trifasciata*, Dewitz, Verh. Leop.-Carol. Akad. xlii. p. 82, pl. 3. fig. 3 (1881).
♀, Mgana, 13th August, 1896; ♂ ♀ ♀, Mombasa, 4th & 7th January, 1897.

#### 133. SECUSIO STRIGATA.

*Secusio strigata*, Walker, Cat. Lep. Het. ii. p. 550 (1864).
Taru, ♀ ♀, 22nd November and 19th December, 1896.

#### 134. LEPTOSOMA LEUCONOE.

*Nyctemera leuconoe*, Hopffer, Monatsber. königl. Akad.Wissensch. Berlin, 1857, p. 422; Peters's Reise n. Mossamb., Ins. p. 430, pl. xxviii. fig. 3 (1862).

Mgana, 22nd June and 12th July; Taru, 19th December, 1896.

#### 135. LEPTOSOMA FALLAX?

*Nyctemera fallax*, Holland, Ent. News Philad. 1893, p. 59.
♂, Taru, 17th January, 1897.

We only have a single female of this species in the Museum collection; the present male does not seem to differ more from it than the sex would account for; but, as the type of *L. fallax* was from the West, I feel no certainty of the specific identity of the two insects.

## AGARISTIDÆ.

#### 136. ÆGOCERA TRICOLOR.

*Ægocera tricolor*, Druce, Ent. Month. Mag. vol. xx. p. 155 (1883).

Samburu, 10th & 15th November, 1896; between Voi and Ndi, 22nd May, 1897.

The last example obtained is of interest on account of the distortion of the subapical patch across the right primary. It seems to me not at all unlikely that this may prove to be only a form of *Æ. leucomelas* with orange secondaries; a similar variation in colouring occurs in the very closely related *Æ. trimeni* and in *Æ. triplagiata*.

## NOCTUIDÆ.

#### 137. EUPLEXIA OPPOSITA.

*Mamestra opposita*, Walker, Cat. Lep. Het. xxxii. p. 667 (1865).

Mbuyuni, 29th May, 1897.

#### 138. AMYNA SELENAMPHA.

*Amyna selenampha*, Guenée, Noct. i. p. 406 (1852).

Samburu, 28th October, 1896.

One rather rubbed example of this abundant species was obtained.

#### 139. TARACHE UPSILON.

*Calophasia upsilon*, Walker, Cat. Lep. Het. xxxiii. p. 763.

Samburu, 2nd November; Taru, 24th November, 1896, 21st January, 1897.

#### 140. TARACHE PORPHYREA, sp. n.

General pattern of both sexes similar to that of *T. tropica*; coloration of primaries nearer to *T. ardoris* but more clouded. Primaries of male with the basal two-thirds bone-whitish, clouded and transversely banded with plumbeous grey, varied with olivaceous; a black spot at end of cell, but none in the cell, the pale area terminating beyond the cell in the usual pale-edged blackish olivaceous ℨ-shaped character impinging upon the external third, which is glistening sepia-brown; the external border faintly indicated excepting at the extremity of the median areoles and at the external angle, where it becomes whitish; the two patches connected internally by a zigzag whitish line; a marginal series of black dots, barely visible excepting upon the pale patches: secondaries silky smoke-brown, a little darker on outer border and slightly cupreous in certain lights. Thorax whitish, more or less varied with greyish; abdomen whitish or grey, that of the female sometimes grey, with the posterior borders of the segments buff.

Wings below glistening grey, the internal area of primaries whitish, the costal border and external margin in the female varied with ochreous; the secondaries in this sex also somewhat paler, slightly yellowish towards costa, especially from the middle, and crossed by an irregular oblique subapical grey band; a dark grey spot at end of cell: body below milk-white, tibiæ and tarsi barred with grey. Expanse of wings 19–20 millim.

♂ ♀, between Voi and Ndi, 88 miles from Mombasa, 4th June, 1897.

In 1884 we received a slightly smaller pair of this species from Accra; but these are all that I have seen of it.

### 141. Tarache sp.

♀. Probably new, but too imperfect to describe; it is nearly related to a very beautiful unnamed female (also from British East Africa) in the Museum collection; but differs in so many details of colouring, that I cannot venture to regard it as a variety of that insect: also, in this genus, in which the sexes often differ to a marvellous degree, it is not satisfactory to describe from a female alone.

♀, between Voi and Ndi, 4th June, 1897.

### 142. Tarache admota.

*Acontia admota,* Felder, Reise der Nov., Lep. v. pl. cviii. fig. 31 (1875).

Samburu, 31st October, 1896.

I have previously seen this insect from extreme North and from South Africa; but it is new to us from East Africa. In fresh examples the markings on the primaries are bright olive-green; the figure in the 'Novara Voyage' is not characteristic.

### 143. Polydesma umbricola.

*Polydesma umbricola,* Boisduval, Faune Ent. de Madag., Lép. p. 108, pl. 13. fig. 5.

♀ ♀, Voi, 2nd May and 16th July; between Voi and Ndi, 18th May, 1897.

Two damaged females of *Ericeia inangulata,* Guen., were obtained at Samburu (Oct. 26th) and Taru (Nov. 28th).

### 144. Cyligramma latona.

*Phalæna (Noctua) latona,* Cramer, Pap. Exot. i. p. 20, pl. xiii. B (1779).

Samburu, 17th & 20th November; Taru, 22nd, 24th, & 28th November, 6th & 9th December, 1896; between Voi and Ndi, 18th May, 1897.

### 145. Cyligramma fluctuosa.

*Phalæna (Noctua) fluctuosa,* Drury, Ill. Exot. Ent. ii. p. 24, pl. xiv. fig. 1.

Var. *Cyligramma rudilinea*, Walker, Cat. Lep. Het. xiv. p. 1311 (1857).

Var. *Cyligramma limacina*, Guérin, Icon. Règne Anim., Ins. pl. 89. fig. 2, texte p. 520.

Mgana, 5th & 6th August : three miles north of Samburu, 23rd October ; Taru, 20th, 22nd, 23rd, 24th, & 28th November, 1896.

Three examples agreeing with *C. limacina*, the remainder intermediate between the latter and *C. rudilinea* ; therefore typical. This form of the species is new to the Museum collection.

### 146. DYSGONIA ABNEGANS, var.

*Ophiusa? abnegans*, Walker, Cat. Lep. Het. xv. p. 1831 (1858).

Mgana, 27th July and 30th August, 1896.

Neither of the two specimens obtained quite agrees with Walker's type from Sierra Leone, though one is nearer than the other. It is very important to secure these aberrant examples, as only thus can we hope to comprehend the variability of the species in this genus (which at times is considerable). I am quite satisfied that *D. neptunia* of Holland is Walker's *D. conjunctura*, and I am not at all certain that *D. palpalis* of Walker is more than a variety of the same species.

In the Eastern specimens of *D. abnegans* before me the band forming the inner limitation of the bicoloured central belt on the primaries is less inarched at costa, though more so in one example than in the other ; the subapical markings vary individually.

### 147. DYSGONIA ANGULARIS.

*Ophiusa angularis*, Boisduval, Faune Ent. de Madag., Lép. p. 103, pl. 13. fig. 2.

Mgana, 27th July, 1896 ; Mombasa, 8th January : between Voi and Ndi, 18th May, 1897.

New to the Museum series from Eastern Africa.

### 148. ACHÆA LIENARDI.

*Ophiusa lienardi*, Boisduval, Faune Ent. de Madag., Lép. p. 102, pl. 15. fig. 5.

Taru, 20th December, 1896.

### 149. GRAMMODES STOLIDA.

*Noctua stolida*, Fabricius, Sp. Ins. ii. p. 218.

Machuma, 21st February, 1897.

New to the Museum from East Africa.

### 150. SPHINGOMORPHA MONTEIRONIS.

*Sphingomorpha monteironis*, Butler, Ann. & Mag. Nat. Hist. ser. 4, vol. xvi. p. 406 (1875).

Mkwajuni, 20th & 21st October ; three miles north of Samburu, 23rd October ; Taru, 6th December, 1896.

151. GNAMPTONYX TREFOLIATA, sp. n.

General aspect of an *Acronycta*, but belonging to the quadrifid group of *Noctuidæ*. Primaries earthy brown, sprinkled all over with pale lavender scales ; an ill-defined, dusky, oblique costal streak entering discoidal cell just above the orbicular spot, which is whitish, outlined in black ; the reniform stigma is represented by a large irregular black-edged marking, not unlike a hawthorn or trefoil leaf with the mid-rib directed inwards to below the orbicular spot ; an oblique costal streak at apical fourth, external border ashy lavender, its inner margin widely and deeply sinuated between costa and first median branch, but diffused below the latter ; a vague indication of a dusky annulus on inner margin near external angle ; a series of small black submarginal spots ; fringe whitish, sprinkled with earthy-brown scales ; secondaries sericeous white with a very faint fleshy tint ; the external area dust greyish ; a marginal series of black dashes ; fringe white at base, greyish externally : head brownish grey, collar less brown, ashy in front and at the sides ; thorax ashy ; abdomen buffish white irrorated with grey. Wings below white, slightly buffish and irrorated with dark brown scales on costal and apical areas ; a marginal series of blackish spots ; secondaries with a dusky spot on upper discocellular : body below sordid buffish white ; front of pectus, palpi and legs above brownish irrorated with blackish, the tarsi with white tips to the joints. Expanse of wings 60 millim.

Between Voi and Ndi, 2nd June, 1897.

Unfortunately only one example of this species was obtained. I am indebted to Sir George Hampson for pointing out its affinities ; despite its dissimilarity from the type of his genus *Gnamptonyx*, it corresponds with it so closely in structure that I have no doubt of its correct location.

152. BANIANA INTORTA.

*Baniana intorta*, Swinhoe, Trans. Ent. Soc. 1891, p. 150 ; Hampson, Ill. Typ. Het. ix. pl. 163. fig. 3.

♀, Taru, 23rd November, 1896.

New to the Museum from Eastern Africa, though we have it from Natal and Accra.

153. COLBUSA PENTAGONALIS.

*Colbusa pentagonalis*, Butler, P. Z. S. 1894, p. 589, pl. xxxvii. fig. 8.

Samburu, 7th November, 1896.

A larger and better example than the type, and therefore a desirable acquisition.

154. TRIGONODES HYPPASIA.

*Phalæna-Noctua hippasia*, Cramer, Pap. Exot. iii. pl. ccl. E (1782).

Mbuyuni, 25th April ; between Voi and Ndi, 20th & 22nd May ; Voi, 26th June, 1897.

155. REMIGIA ARCHESIA.

*Phalæna-Noctua archesia*, Cramer, Pap. Exot. iii. p. 145,
pl. cclxxiii. F, G (1782).
Mgana, 27th July and 18th August, 1896.

156. REMIGIA REPANDA.

*Noctua repanda*, Fabricius, Ent. Syst. iii. 2, p. 49 (1793).
Mgana, 27th July, 20th, 27th, & 30th August, 1896.

157. ENTOMOGRAMMA NIGRICEPS.

*Renodes ? nigriceps*, Walker, Cat. Lep. Het. xv. p. 1595 (1858).
Mgana, 5th August, 1896.

158. OPHIODES FINIFASCIA.

*Nephelodes finifascia*, Walker, Cat. Lep. Het. xv. p. 1676 (1858).
Taru, 4th February, 1897.
One imperfect example.

159. PASIPEDA ROSEIVENTRIS.

*Asymbata roseiventris*, Gerstaecker, in Von der Decken's Reisen
in Ost-Afrika, iii. 2, p. 378, pl. xv. fig. 8 (1873).
♂, Voi, 30th April; ♀, between Voi and Ndi, 4th June, 1897.
The male is the first example of that sex which I have seen;
the species seems to be rare, though nearly related to the common
Indian *P. satellitia*; possibly it has simply not been collected.

160. HALASTUS DIVITIOSUS.

*Ophideres divitiosa*, Walker, Proc. Nat. Hist. Soc. Glasgow, vol. i.
p. 356, pl. vii. fig. 11 (1869).
Machuma, 22nd February, 1897.

161. ARGADESA MATERNA.

*Phalæna-Noctua materna*, Linnæus, Syst. Nat. ii. p. 840 (1767).
♂, Samburu, 15th November, 1896 ; ♀, Maungu Inkubwa, 21st
March, 1897.

162. COSMOPHILA EROSA.

*Anomis erosa*, Hübner, Exot. Schmett. Zutr. ii. p. 19, figs. 287,
288.
♀, Samburu, 16th November, 1896.

163. HYPOCALA DEFLORATA, var. PLUMICORNIS.

*Hypocala plumicornis*, Guenée, Noct. iii. p. 75 (1852).
Samburu, 14th November, 1896.

164. PLUSIA ERIOSOMA.

*Plusia eriosoma*, Doubleday in Dieffenbach's New Zealand, i.
p. 285 (1843).

Samburu, 7th, 8th, & 16th November; Taru, 22nd November & 20th December, 1896.

This abundant species seems to be almost cosmopolitan.

### 165. RISOBA OBSTRUCTA.

*Risoba obstructa*, Moore, P. Z. S. 1881, p. 328; Lep. Ceylon, iii. p. 2, pl. cxliv. figs. 2, 2 *a*, 2 *b* (1884).

Samburu, 2nd November, 1896.

This is quite new to the African fauna.

### 166. GONITIS SABULIFERA.

*Gonitis sabulifera*, Guenée, Noct. ii. p. 404 (1852).

Mgana, 30th August; Samburu, 31st October, 4th & 7th November; Taru, 24th, 27th, & 28th November, 9th December, 1896.

Many of the specimens belong to the variety named by Walker *G. involuta*. The species is new to us from East Africa, though we have it both from Abyssinia and Natal.

### 167. MARASMALUS DISCISTRIGA.

*Eutelia discitriga* (sic), Walker, Cat. Lep. Het. xxxiii. p. 823 (1865).

Samburu, 4th November; Taru, 1st December, 1896.

I have never previously seen this species from Eastern Africa, but we have it from Aden, and therefore it probably is to be found in the extreme North.

### 168. ZETHES BETTONI, sp. n.

Closely allied to *Z. hesperioides*, having exactly the same outline, structure, and nearly the same pattern; it is, however, distinctly smaller; the peculiar hatchet-shaped central belt across the primaries is pale buffish, flesh-tinted or greyish, with the borders of the lower half very black in fresh specimens; the pale costal dots are sometimes much whiter than in the species from Java and Burma, and the subquadrate costal patch towards apex paler and therefore less prominent; the submarginal line on all the wings is whitish with dark brown borders; on the under surface the resemblance to *Z. hesperioides* is again very great, but the basal area is paler, the narrow dark-bordered transverse central band usually paler, sometimes quite white, the discal belt sometimes much darker than in any specimens of the larger species. Expanse of wings, ♂ 31–32 millim., ♀ 29–32 millim.

Taru, 1st, 6th, & 9th December, 1896.

### 169. EGNASIA VICARIA.

*Thyridospila vicaria*, Walker, Cat. Lep. Het. xxxv. p. 1972 (1866).

Mgana, 1st August, 1896.

### 170. RAPARNA LIMBATA, sp. n.

♀. Primaries above pale coffee reddish, sericeous; the costal border whity brown ; external border narrowly and unevenly pale grey-brownish bounded internally by a partly zigzag, partly widely sinuous, white submarginal line, the latter bounded internally towards apex and towards external angle by a diffused dusky patch ; central area of wing enclosed by two indistinct crenulated grey lines, the inner one interrupted in the cell by a white ' orbicular ' dot ; reniform stigma also white, partly edged with leaden grey ; a marginal series of black dots : secondaries pale smoky brown, sericeous, slightly greyer towards outer margin ; fringes of all the wings grey inclining to blackish, with whity-brown basal line.    Head and collar whity brown, somewhat pearly ; thorax flesh-reddish ; abdomen whity brown.    Under surface sericeous whity brown, the wings irrorated with greyish and with dusky marginal dots. Expanse of wings 25 millim.

Taru, 2nd February, 1897.

Unfortunately only one example of this very distinct species was obtained.

### 171. HYPENA VULGATALIS.

*Hypena vulgatalis*, Walker, Cat. Lep. Het. xvi. p. 82 (1858).

Samburu, 2nd November, 1896.

A single somewhat worn specimen, but new to us from Eastern Africa.

### 172. OPHIUCHE MASURIALIS.

*Hypena masurialis*, Guenée, Delt. et Pyral. p. 38 (1854).

Samburu, 8th & 12th November, 1896.

New to us from East Africa, though we have it from the North, South, and West.

### 173. RHYNCHINA TARUENSIS, sp. n.

Intermediate in character between *R. plusioides* and *R. antiqualis*, nearest to the latter, slightly larger and browner ; a black or dark brown patch filling the interval between the black orbicular spot and the linear white ' reniform stigma,' and a second smaller black spot filling the angle of the inner angulated white transverse line : the costal and discal black spots of *R. antiqualis* almost or wholly obliterated : no irregular submarginal white line as in that species, but the external border faintly dusted with ashy-white scales ; marginal line brown, scarcely discernible : in other respects the two species are almost identical.    Expanse of wings 25–26 millim.

Taru, 27th & 29th November, 1st December, 1896.

### 174. NODARIA EXTERNALIS.

*Nodaria externalis*, Guenée, Delt. et Pyral. p. 64 (1854).

♀, between Voi and Ndi, 16th May, 1897.

175. SIMPLICIA INFLEXALIS.

*Simplicia inflexalis,* Guenée, Delt. et Pyral. p. 52 (1854).

Samburu, 31st October, 1896; between Voi and Ndi, 19th May, 1897.

New to us from East Africa.

One other Noctuid was obtained at Taru on December 1st, 1896, but it is headless and rubbed, so that its identification is impossible.

## LYMANTRIIDÆ.

176. REDOA CROCIPES.

*Cypra crocipes,* Boisduval, Faune Ent. de Madag. p. 87, pl. 12. fig. 2.

♀, Maungu Inkubwa, 21st March, 1897.

The female is quite new to us; unfortunately only one example was obtained.

177. CROPERA TESTACEA.

*Cropera testacea,* Walker, Cat. Lep. Het. iv. p. 826 (1855).

♀ ♀, Mgana, 18th & 30th June, 1896; Voi, 7th May, 1897.
New to us from East Africa.

178. OGOA SIMPLEX.

*Ogoa simplex,* Walker, Cat. Lep. Het. vii. p. 1764 (1856).

♀, Taru, 19th December, 1896.

The type (the only other example which I have seen) is from Natal; this is therefore a welcome addition to the Museum collection.

179. LACIPA IMPUNCTA, sp. n.   (Plate XXXII. fig. 6.)

Allied to *L. gracilis* : silvery white; primaries of the male with a pale buff spot and black dot near base of costa, and angular series of orange spots before the middle, of which the four lower ones are conspicuous, and a slightly sigmoidal (*geschwungen* [1]) oblique series of seven spots across the disc; head, collar, and pterygodes pale buff; antennal pectinations testaceous; abdomen golden buff. Expanse of wings 23 millim.

The female, which I formerly supposed to be a variety of *L. gracilis,* was obtained in the Sabaki Valley by Dr. Gregory: it has no basi-costal spots on the primaries; the inner series of orange spots is reduced to two, and the outer series to six, all small; the body is white, with blackish anal tuft. Expanse of wings 35 millim.

♂, Mgana, 31st August, 1896.

The absence of all the black spots characteristic of *L. gracilis,* the nearer approach of the discal series of orange spots to the

[1] We have no English equivalent for this word, which exactly expresses the barely perceptible S-character of a line; 'sinuous' might mean more than S-shaped.

outer margin, the shorter fringe, and the deeper colouring of the male abdomen, readily distinguish this species from Hopffer's *L. gracilis.*

180. LOPERA MONOSTICTA, sp. n. (Plate XXXII. fig. 7.)

Nearest to *L. pallida,* Kirby, but the primaries creamy white, with a single small orange spot at the end of the cell; secondaries sericeous, snow-white; head ochreous; antennæ white, with testaceous pectinations; front of thorax, including the collar and anterior two-thirds of pterygodes, creamy white, remainder of body snow-white; under surface white; the basal half of costal margin of primaries buff; the collar below and the anterior coxæ ochreous. Expanse of wings 27 millim.

♂, Taru, 19th December, 1896.

181. ILEMA ROBUSTA?

*Acyphas robusta,* Walker, Cat. Lep. Het. iv. p. 799 (1855).

♂, Taru, 23rd November, 1896.

A fragment, much rubbed, apparently referable to this species.

ACLONOPHLEBIA, gen. nov.

Near to *Euproctis,* but totally dissimilar in aspect, altogether far less woolly; the head much more prominent, the palpi short, but very broadly fringed; pectinations of antennæ much coarser; legs much less hairy, the hind tibiæ with only the terminal pair of spurs, which are much more conical; the neuration very similar, but the subcostal veins of the secondaries (veins 6 and 7) not emitted from a footstalk, but near together from the anterior angle of the cell. Type *A. flavinotata.*

182. ACLONOPHLEBIA FLAVINOTATA, sp. n. (Plate XXXII. fig. 8.)

♀. Primaries above lilacine grey clouded with brown; a regular biangulated dark brown line across the middle of the wing, bordered broadly inside with whitish and outside with brownish; costal and interno-basal borders brownish; sometimes a black spot in the cell; a large diffused chrome-yellow patch beyond the lower angle of the cell, and a line of the same colour edging the central angulated line between its alternate angles; fringe pale stramineous indistinctly spotted with brownish: secondaries pale stramineous. Thorax grey; head, collar, and patagia clothed with testaceous hairs; antennæ grey, with darker pectinations; abdomen fulvous. Under surface stramineous, costal borders of wings ochraceous; primaries with a greyish spot at end of cell, indicating part of the central band of the upper surface; tarsi with greyish bands. Expanse of wings 27–32 millim.

Marago ya Fundi, 1st March; between Voi and Ndi, 2nd June, 1897.

Unfortunately only two examples, varying in size and also differing somewhat in pattern, were obtained.

## HYPSIDÆ.

### 183. EGYBOLIA VAILLANTINA.

*Phalæna vaillantina*, Stoll, Suppl. Cramer, Pap. Exot. v. p. 142, pl. xxxi. fig. 3.

Mgana, 30th August, 1896; Mombasa, 4th January, 1897.
It is not at all certain that this is a true Hypsid.

### 184. SOMMERIA CULTA.

*Sommeria culta*, Hübner, Exot. Schmett. Zutr. figs. 433, 434 (1818).

♂ ♀, Samburu, 1st & 5th November, 1896.
This is an interesting variety in which the normal white markings on the primaries are suffused with the ground-colour, giving them a very uniform character. That this is mere variation and has no specific value is evident from the fact that we have an example in the Museum in which the left primary is similarly suffused, whilst on the right primary many of the white markings are present.

## SATURNIIDÆ.

### 185. USTA WALLENGRENII.

*Saturnia wallengrenii*, Felder, Wien. ent. Monatschr. iii. p. 323, pl. vi. fig. 2.

♀, Maungu Inkubwa, 29th March, 1897.
This is the only fairly perfect example I have ever seen—the species having hitherto only reached us from Dr. Gregory's collection, and so much rubbed and shattered as to be barely recognizable. Unless Felder had a very closely allied species, his figure is incorrect (probably made up from an injured specimen, as the outer black edging to the central belt of the primaries is deeply and conically incised between veins 2 and 3).

### 186. BUNÆA (THYELLA) ZAMBESIA.

*Thyella zambesia*, Felder, Reise der Nov., Lep. ii. pl. lxxxv. fig. 5 (1874).

♂, Taru, 30th March, 1897.
The larva of this moth (which is quite new to the Museum Collection) is said by Mr. Betton to have been common at Taru on December 10th; the present example pupated on December 17th, 1896, and emerged at the end of the following March. The larvæ and pupa, which Mr. Betton preserved, were unfortunately not sent to us with his collection; he refers to the former as "bottle of larvæ marked Taru, Nov. 23 to Dec. 15, 1896," and to the latter—" see matchbox marked 'M.'"

If Mr. Betton could breed a series of this Saturniid, I think it would be conclusively proved that *B. barcas* Maassen was only a variation; it certainly is extremely closely related, if distinct, and the fact that both occur at Zanzibar is very suspicious.

187. HENUCHA HANSALII?

*Ludia hansalii*, Felder, Reise der Nov., Lep. ii. pl. lxxxix. fig. 1 (1874).

♀, Voi, 22nd April, 1897.

Felder's figure is either extremely bad, or this is a new species; it is very probable that the former is the correct explanation of the differences which exist between the two, and that the illustration was taken from a frayed and faded male. The species is quite new to the Museum, though nearly allied to the southern *H. delegorguei*, from which it differs chiefly in the trisinuated inner margin of the central belt of the primaries, its regularly undulated outer edging, the white margin of which is emphasized by a grey-mottled series of very indistinct markings across the disc. The female has the outer margins of the wings even more distinctly dentated than in that sex of *H. delegorguei*, but it is probable that this may not be the case in the male.

188. GOODIA HOLLANDI, sp. n.    (Plate XXXIII. fig. 1.)

Allied to *G. nubilata*, but considerably smaller and paler: the male pale buff: the primaries clouded with fawn towards base of costa, the discoidal cell and centre of costa whitish, slightly mottled with lilacine grey (but most distinctly on costa); an ill-defined, irregular, transverse, dusky line across basal fourth, beyond which the inner border is partly white, flecked and edged with black almost to external angle; an oblique, ill-defined, sub-angulated, brown median band, just crossing the posterior angle of the discoidal cell and almost merging with a very broad golden-brown apical area crossed by an oblique slender dentate-sinuate black line, edged externally with whitish buff; costal border towards apex rose-tinted; the centre of external area occupied by a diffused lilacine greyish nebula, which commences in a dark grey cuneiform patch on outer margin towards apex: a curved blackish line on lower discocellular followed above the base of vein 4 by a buff-whitish spot: secondaries somewhat tawny within and below discoidal cell; a dusky line on discocellulars; an arched dentate-sinuate dusky line, blackish near inner margin, crossing the disc parallel to outer margin; costal and external areas pearly, tinted with pale rose and grey; inner or abdominal margin mottled with whitish and black. Head purplish brown, collar white, ochreous at sides, and brown-edged; thorax and base of abdomen pale buff; remainder of abdomen ruddy brown, excepting the anal tuft which is ochraceous; antennæ dark brown, with double divergent bipectinations fringed with buff-whitish pile. Under surface differing a good deal in detail from the upper surface, brown mottled and heavily clouded with lilacine greyish on basal half; body rosy brownish-purplish in front. Expanse of wings 58 millim.

♀. Smaller and altogether more ash-coloured than the male; the primaries less falcate, the secondaries narrower, less produced at anal angle, most of the markings obliterated, but the cell of the primaries ashy whitish as well as the area below it.  Expanse of wings 53 millim.

♂, Voi, 18th April, 1897; ♀, Yaru, from larva obtained 12th December, 1896, pupated 20th December, emerged 4th May, 1897.

The species is also related to *Lasioptila ansorgei* Kirby (=*Saturnia kuntzei* Dewitz), which must be referred to Dr. Holland's genus *Goodia*.  Kirby's *L. pomona* is not congeneric with the latter; therefore if his generic name is retained it must take *L. pomona* as type, instead of *L. ansorgei*.

I have named this pretty little species after the learned author of the genus, to whom all students of African Lepidoptera owe a debt of gratitude for his admirable work.


## EUPTEROTIDÆ.

### TROTONOTUS, gen. nov.

Allied to *Gangarides*, but with the form and aspect of *Eutricha* (*Lasiocampidæ*): the primaries not falcate, the radial of the secondaries (vein 5) wanting, only indicated by a fold, which disappears when damped with benzine; the angles of the cell also almost parallel; veins 6 and 7 not stalked as in *Gangarides*; the neuration of the primaries is practically the same in the two genera; the palpi are narrower, less densely fringed, the antennæ bipectinated almost to the tips; the abdomen much shorter and conical rather than truncated at the anal extremity, with expansive lateral tufts; the legs very hairy; middle and hind tibiæ with strong pointed terminal spurs, the hind tibiæ also with a second subterminal pair of spurs.  Type *T. bettoni*.

### 189. TROTONOTUS BETTONI, sp. n.     (Plate XXXIII. fig. 2.)

♂.  Primaries above coffee-brown, faintly glossed here and there with glaucous;  a rose-and-white tufted ochre-yellow spot below base of cell;  an irregularly undulated, partly interrupted, internally blackish-edged yellow ʒ-shaped band across the basal third, also a few scattered yellow spots near its inner edge; a small deep ochreous reniform stigma;  a broad internally angulated and undulated, externally irregular and sinuated discal yellow belt, traversed by four parallel dentate-sinuate stripes of the ground-colour and bordered outside by a blackish stripe;  an oblique increasing slaty-blackish streak from apex, continuous with four transverse patches of the same colour parallel to outer margin;  fringe darker than the rest of the ground-colour and tipped with blackish:  secondaries pale ruddy-chestnut, shading into bone-yellowish on basi-costal area;  fringe tipped with snow-white.  Thorax greyish chocolate, with the top of the head, two large subconfluent spots on the middle of the collar, and the dorsal portion of the thorax between the patagia bright brick-red;  antennæ pale buff, with white basal tuft and golden-brown

29*

pectinations ; abdomen pale ruddy chestnut, more golden towards the base, and with pure white lateral and anal tufts. Under surface white ; the wings slightly yellowish on costal area ; the apical and external areas of all the wings minutely dusted with coffee-colour ; the secondaries, excepting along abdominal border, purer white than the primaries; pectus buffish at the sides, the anterior legs bright coffee-coloured in front, the second pair slightly stained and the third pair irrorated with the same colour ; venter more densely and finely irrorated. Expanse of wings 49 millim.

Mgana, 28th August, 1896.

It is unfortunate that Mr. Betton was only able to secure one male of this strikingly beautiful new form ; the specimen, however, is in good condition and will be a most welcome addition to the Museum collection.

### 190. SABALIA PICARINA.

*Sabalia picarina*, Walker, Cat. Lep. Het. xxxii. p. 548 (1865).

Samburu, 13th November, 1896.

Unfortunately only one somewhat broken example was obtained ; it is a species badly represented in the Museum collection, of which we should be glad to obtain good specimens.

### SPHINGIDÆ.

### 191. LOPHOSTETHUS DEMOLINII.

*Sphinx demolinii*, Angas, Kaffirs Illustrated, pl. xxx. fig. 11 (1849).

♂, Taru, 29th November, 1896 ; ♀, Voi, 17th April, 1897.

### 192. POLYPTYCHUS GRAYII.

*Smerinthus grayii*, Walker, Cat. Lep. Het. viii. p. 249 (1856).

♀, Voi, pupa 6th May, emerged 12th May ; ♀, Mbuyuni, 30th May, 1897.

We previously only possessed the male of this species, from Natal.

### 193. DIODOSIDA ROSEIPENNIS.

*Diodosida roseipennis*, Butler, Ann. & Mag. Nat. Hist. ser. 5, vol. x. p. 433 (1882).

♂ ♂, Maungu Inkubwa, 31st March ; Voi, 7th May, 1897.

The male is new to the Museum, the type being a female from Delagoa Bay.

### 194. PROTOPARCE CONVOLVULI.

*Sphinx convolvuli*, Linnæus, Syst. Nat. 1, ii. p. 789 (1766).

Voi, 7th May, 1897.

### 195. AELLOPUS HIRUNDO.

*Macroglossa hirundo*, Gerstaecker, Arch. Nat. xxxvii. p. 360

(1871) ; Von der Decken's Reisen in Ost-Africa, Gliederthiere, p. 375, pl. xv. fig. 7 (1873).

Maungu Inkubwa, 21st March, 1897.

## NOTODONTIDÆ.

### 196. ANTHEUA SIMPLEX.

*Antheua simplex*, Walker, Cat. Lep. Het. iii. p. 687 (1855).

♀, Taru, 23rd November, 1896.

The female is quite new to us and is of considerable interest, as it clearly indicates that *A. cinerea* Walk. is the female of *A. spurcata* of the same author.

### 197. STAUROPUS DASYCHIROIDES, sp. n. (Plate XXXII. fig. 12.)

♀. Primaries pale lilacine ash-grey, orbicular and reniform spots buffish white, ill-defined; a vague oblique dusky stripe from costa just behind the orbicular spot, uniting below first median branch with an ill-defined, pale-buff-bordered, undulated, arched post-median dusky line; beyond the latter three almost parallel diffused stripes, which form an imperfect widely zigzag inner limitation to a slightly paler external border; costa crossed beyond the middle by three or four short dusky bars: secondaries semitransparent white, with sordid costal border and moderately broad smoky-brown outer border; fringe ashy white: antennæ rosy cupreous, with ferruginous pectinations; thorax coloured like the primaries, the patagia slightly brownish; abdomen pale brownish ash. Primaries below pale lilacine ash-coloured, with vague whitish orbicular and reniform spots, between which runs a grey oblique streak from the costa; a faint trace of a postmedian stripe commencing in an oblique blackish costal dash, three blackish subapical costal spots, below which a broad smoky submarginal belt commences and runs to external angle; outer border pale lilacine ash-grey; interno-basal area white : secondaries as above: pectus ashy; legs somewhat fuliginous; venter sordid white. Expanse of wings 53 millim.

Maziwa Mitatu, 27th March, 1897.

This curious species has the neuration of *Stauropus*, but does not nearly resemble any form know to me.

## GEOMETRIDÆ.

### 198. GONODELA SUFFLATA.

*Macaria sufflata*, Guenée, Phal. ii. p. 88, pl. xvii. fig. 8.

Between Voi and Ndi, 3rd & 4th June, 1897.

New to the Museum from East Africa, though we have it from the extreme south and from Abyssinia.

### 199. CŒNINA AURIVENA, sp. n.

*Cœnina flavivena* Warren, MS.

♀. Primaries formed as in *C. pœcilaria*, pale greyish stone-brown; the discoidal cell and a streak beyond it as well as the internal area mottled with cream-whitish, and the whole surface irrorated with blackish dots; a dusky almost falciform postmedian stripe; external angle mottled along inner margin with ferruginous; fringe white, varied with greyish brown at base: secondaries with deeply but widely inarched costa; outer margin produced into an acute point at extremity of first subcostal branch and very slightly sinuated between the apex and this point; remainder of outer margin slightly inarched, and very slightly sinuated to the so-called 'third median branch,' otherwise very regular; costal half coloured like the primaries, internal half almost to submedian vein suffused with coffee-brown, ferruginous at anal angle; a triangular yellow patch edged and intersected by ferruginous lines at base of median veins, and a short tapering white bar (in continuation of the yellow patch) across the end of the cell; abdominal area creamy white varying to silvery white; fringe white; the surface of the wing irrorated with blackish dots like that of the primaries. Head and palpi orange; antennæ cream-white; remainder of body above coloured like the primaries. Under surface of wings paler than above, mottled with deeper grey and speckled with black; the primaries with a longitudinal streak beyond the cell, a spot at base of median interspace and the interno-basal three-fifths creamy white grey-mottled; a subapical diffused patch, a patch below the centre of the disc, a very irregular patch at external angle, and a portion of the veins from the median backwards orange-tawny: secondaries with the abdominal half white, the costal half blotched and veined with orange-tawny; a white bar beyond the discoidal cell as above; outer margin grey varied with orange-tawny; fringe white: body below pale greyish brown, almost white on venter; legs varied with ferruginous.  Expanse of wings 34 to 37 millim.

Samburu, 3rd November, 1896; Mbuyuni, 29th May, 1897.

We have males in the Museum from Ambriz and Accra; they show a tawny or brown-edged spot at the base of the median branches of the primaries above, more distinctly than in the female (where it only appears like an excrescence of the discoidal streak); the median vein and base of the submedian vein in the example from Ambriz are also yellowish (which doubtless suggested Warren's unsatisfactory name for the species). The darker portion of the secondaries in specimens from Accra is also darker in both sexes than in the male from Angola, but this is doubtless a variable character; the pectinations of the antennæ in male examples are pale orange.

The veins on the under surface of the primaries being partly orange-tawny, I have modified the manuscript name proposed by Warren.


200. A Boarmian form too much injured for identification, being not only faded and broken but a female.

Voi, 16th April, 1897.

## HAMEOPIS, gen. nov.

Apparently nearer to *Zamacra* than to any other Geometrid genus, though differing entirely in neuration, in body clothing, in character of legs and palpi. Wings broader, shorter, and utterly dissimilar in character : primaries with veins 8 and 9 out of 7, stalked ; 10 and 11 closely approximated, stalked at base : secondaries with all the veins separate excepting 7 and 8, which coalesce close to base, separating again before middle of cell ; veins 3 and 7 both emitted from cell before the terminal angles. Antennæ with long straggling pectinations (as in *Zamacra*) to about four-fifths of the distance from their base, terminal fifth serrated ; palpi small, porrected, smooth ; thorax coarsely scaled, but not hairy ; frontal process prominent, subquadrate, with bare $\Lambda$-shaped ridge running between the antennæ to back of head and deep facial depression ; legs smooth ; hind tibiæ with median spurs emitted close behind the terminal pair. Type *H. rudicornis.*

### 201. HAMEOPIS RUDICORNIS, sp. n. (Plate XXXII. fig. 13.)

Wings above sericeous white ; primaries irregularly speckled all over with grey and blackish, a mottled subbasal band angulated at median vein, a reversed oblique costal spot just beyond middle, an oblique discal band forked ou costa, and a partial outer border of the same colours, the blackish parts being costal : secondaries with a few scattered dark grey dots chiefly on the veins, indicating a discal transverse line ; an apical patch and some scattered clusters of dots representing an external border. Head and thorax white, the horny shovel-shaped process and forked dorsal ridge on the head deep chestnut ; shaft of antennæ dark smoke-grey, white barred with dark grey at base, pectinations pale brownish grey ; thorax white, patagia alternately spotted and transversely barred with black, metathorax similarly marked ; abdomen golden testaceous, whitish at the sides and at anal extremity, with dorsal dusky spots. Under surface white : wings paler in markings but otherwise as above ; tibiæ banded in front with grey, tarsi black above. Expanse of wings 42 millim.

♂, Taru, 1st December, 1896.

### 202. HÆMATORITHRA RUBRIFASCIATA.

♂. *Hæmatorithra rubrifasciata*, Butler, Ann. & Mag. Nat. Hist. ser. 6, vol. xviii. p. 162 (1896).

♀, Mgana, 4th August, 1896.

This is the first female I have seen of *H. rubrifasciata* ; the species would seem to be rare, Mr. Crawshay having only obtained two males during his sojourn in Nyasaland.

### 203. PROBLEPSIS VESTALIS.

*Argyris vestalis*, Butler, Ann. & Mag. Nat. Hist. ser. 4, vol. xvi. p. 419 (1875).

Taru, 19th December, 1896.

## LASIOCAMPIDÆ.

### 204. HETEROPACHA sp.

A single female practically agreeing in structure and general appearance with the Texan *H. rileyana*, but too much worn for the pattern to be critically compared.

♀, between Voi and Ndi, 2nd June, 1897.

The specimen is an interesting addition, in spite of its poor condition, on account of its evident close affinity to a New World species.

### 205. CHILENA PROMPTA.

*Lasiocampa prompta*, Walker, Cat. Lep. Het. vi. p. 1437 (1855).
Voi, 22nd & 29th April, 1897.
New to the Museum from Eastern Africa.

### 206. CHILENA DONALDSONI.

*Chilena donaldsoni*, Holland, Through Unknown African Countries, pp. 413 & 420, fig. 8 (1897).

Samburu, 7th November; Taru, 29th November, 1896; Marago ya Fundi, 1st March; between Voi and Ndi, 18th May, 1897.

Fresh examples are darker coloured than the typical form (which was evidently somewhat faded); the silvery white marking on the primaries also sometimes is continued back completely to the base, though the basal half is less purely white than the permanent marking. *C. donaldsoni* is new to the Museum collection.

### 207. LEBEDA KÖLLIKERII.

*Lasiocampa köllikerii*, Dewitz, Verhandl. kais. Leop.-Carol. Deutsch. Akad. Naturf. vol. xlii. p. 78, pl. i. fig. 15 (1881).

♀, Maziwa Mitatu, 18th March, 1897.

The female is quite new to the Museum : structurally it perfectly agrees with *Lebeda nobilis*. A single male from Delagoa Bay was received in 1893, but is so much more yellow and altogether brighter in colour than the female that it was not recognized as Dewitz's species; it also differs in having the body above glistening golden buff, with a large black dorsal patch extending from the base to the anal segment.

## LIMACODIDÆ.

### 208. SCOTINOCHROA INCONSEQUENS.

*Scotinochroa inconsequens*, Butler, P. Z. S. 1896, p. 845.
Maziwa Mitatu, 24th March, 1897.

A single worn and very dirty male specimen, which must, I think, be referable to this species, but differs in having a pale buff patch with reddish centre at external angle of primaries; otherwise it agrees in pattern with the type : it is interesting as a variety.

*Scotinochroa* is very closely related to *Zinara*, Walk.

209. OMOCENA SYRTIS ?

♂. *Miresa syrtis*, Schaus & Clements, Coll. Sierra Leone Lep. p. 28, pl. ii. fig. 3 (1893).

♀, Voi, 19th September, 1897.

The lines across the primaries approximate on costa and diverge more widely on inner margin than in the figure of the male; but variations of this nature are so common, that I dare not venture to assume their importance in the present instance.

210. GAVARA VELUTINA.

♂. *Gavara velutina*, Walker, Cat. Lep. Het. xii. p. 771 (1857).

♀, Maungu Inkubwa, 20th March, 1897.

New to us from E. Africa. Walker placed it in the *Noctuidæ*, just in front of the *Acontiinæ*, to which (of course) it has no affinity.

211. NIPHADOLEPIS AURICINCTA, sp. n.   (Plate XXXII. fig. 9.)

Sericeous snow-white; primaries with faint traces of buff (possibly the indications of a subbasal stripe) near the base; two buff central stripes, oblique and tolerably wide apart from costa to median vein, thence rather closer together and undulated to inner margin; a buff discocellular lunule joining the outer stripe; an abbreviated buff submarginal stripe towards external angle; three black marginal dots at apex and one near to external angle: secondaries with narrow diffused dusky border: collar and patagia stained with buff; abdomen with bright golden-orange hind margins to the segments. Under surface sericeous snow-white, the primaries with sordid buffish suffusion on costal half; all the wings with two blackish marginal dots at apex; anterior legs banded with olive-brown. Expanse of wings 24 millim.

Taru, 29th November, 1896.

*Niphadolepis* approaches *Gavara* in structure, the antennæ and palpi being similar and the venation not very greatly differing.

212. PARYPHANTA BISECTA, sp. n.   (Plate XXXII. fig. 10.)

Nearly allied to *P. fimbriata*: smoky grey, the primaries considerably darker than the secondaries and divided through the middle by a narrow oblique faintly angulated belt, white internally, flesh-tinted externally; a pale submarginal line: fringe with a buffish basal line and pale tips: secondaries bone-whitish towards base; fringe paler than in primaries, but similarly coloured: head pale buffish, antennæ and palpi pale golden ochreous; thorax whity brown, with dusky central transverse belt and posterior margin; abdomen golden-testaceous, with sericeous ashy dorsal transverse bars: under surface pale sandy brownish; primaries sericeous greyish shading to bronze-brown. Expanse of wings 17 millim.

♂, Samburu, 14th November, 1896.

Karsch describes his species as having the primaries grey, densely covered with brown dots; if examined under a platyscopic lens, my species might be described as pale grey densely covered with blackish dots.

## LEMBOPTERIS, gen. nov.

In outline approaching *Tortricidia*, but in coloration and structure perhaps nearer to *Niphadolepis*; the antennæ and palpi smooth, the former submoniliform and feebly setulose from before the middle to the distal extremities; hind tibiæ with very long spurs: primaries with the costal margin long, slightly arched; outer margin very oblique, forming a regular curve with the inner margin which is much arched; veins 7, 8, and 9 stalked: secondaries ovate; veins 3 and 4 from same point; discocellulars deeply inangled; veins 6 and 7 with a short footstalk.  Type *L. puella*.

### 213. LEMBOPTERIS PUELLA, sp. n.  (Plate XXXII. fig. 11.)

Primaries above sericeous snow-white; costal margin narrowly ochreous; two black dots at apex and two on the disc, of which one is below vein 2 and the other (which is not always present) below vein 6: secondaries pale golden stramineous, sericeous, with one dusky marginal dot near apex; fringe white-tipped: head and thorax snow-white; antennæ and palpi golden stramineous; abdomen stramineous, becoming white at base and with olivaceous transverse dorsal bars.   Primaries below stramineous, finely dusted with greyish; fringe white; two blackish apical dots : secondaries sericeous white, almost silvery, costa washed with stramineous; extreme margin indicated by an extremely slender dusky line; a black subapical dot: body below silvery white, the anterior legs and the tarsi and spurs of the remaining legs golden stramineous; venter slightly tinted with this colour.  Expanse of wings 21 millim.

Samburu, 7th November, 1896.

Two somewhat imperfect examples were obtained; apart from the outline of the primaries, the long slender legs and the great length of the median and terminal spurs on the hind pair are very characteristic.

### ARBELIDÆ.

### 214. ARBELA ALBONOTATA, sp. n.

♂. Primaries above ash-grey, varying to whity brown at base, on costa, at external angle, and more or less on inner margin, and with two longitudinal diffused streaks of buffish and chestnut, one short beyond the cell, the other long below the median vein; veins and numerous black-edged transverse striæ sordid white; six pure white spots, one fairly large at end of cell, one small beyond it near outer margin; the other four, are within the interno-median area, each placed upon a transverse stria, the first two small, the last two large and forming a triangle with the spot first mentioned : secondaries sericeous white, veins and margins brownish : antennæ castaneous, the shaft covered with glistening silvery scales; thorax buffish, the borders of all the divisions washed with chestnut and edged with blue-black scales; abdomen clothed with long glistening white hair, the anal extremity with brown-tipped spatulate hair-scales; a large dorsal tuft tipped with blue-black near the base; remaining segments with transverse blue-black bars. Under surface white; markings of upper surface indicated in smoky brownish: secondaries with indications of similar markings on costa and (more vaguely) beyond the middle: body stained in the middle with chestnut brownish; front of head brown; two anterior pairs of legs clothed with brown and blue-black tipped bristles; hind pair less varied in colouring. Expanse of wings 25 to 31 millim.

♂ ♂, Maungu Inkubwa, 2nd April; Mbuyuni Hill, 31st July and 3rd August, 1897.

The example first obtained is somewhat shattered and worn; it represents the greatest expanse of wing and is the palest specimen of the three.

At first I imagined that this species might be the male of Karsch's *Pettigramma spiculata*; but a careful study of his description has satisfied me that his insect is the female of Walker's *Salagena transversa*, from Sierra Leone. *Salagena* differs chiefly from *Arbela* in the upright hair on the anal segment instead of spatulate hair-scales.

## ZYGÆNIDÆ.

### 215. ARNIOCERA CHRYSOSTICTA, sp. n. (Plate XXXIII. fig. 3.)

Allied to *A. auriguttata* (*A. melanopyga* Wallgr.). Wings black, shot with blue; primaries with purplish blue almost to outer margin, where it shades into bright Prussian blue; costa densely irrorated with metallic emerald-green; five golden-ochreous spots as follows—one small, across the cell near its extremity, a larger oval one beyond the cell, one smaller (rounded) between veins 2 and 3, one large at centre of interno-median interspace, and one equally large, subtriangular, very metallic, crossed by vein 1 towards the base: secondaries shot with Antwerp blue, purplish on the fringe. Body black; vertex of head and palpi carmine-red; antennæ shining black; thorax slightly sprinkled with metallic green scales; patagia brilliantly brassy green; metathorax and base of abdomen greenish steel-blue; two terminal segments of abdomen ultramarine-blue, with black anal tuft. Wings below more brightly shot with blue than above, but the submedian golden-ochreous spots partially obliterated; the three others nearly as above. Body below black, the venter brilliantly glossed with steel-blue; anterior legs black externally, but clothed internally with short bright ochreous hair; femora of second pair purplish black, ochreous in front; the tibiæ orange-vermilion externally, clothed internally with long carmine hair; tarsi black; posterior femora purplish black; tibiæ vermilion-red, tipped with blue-black and with a long pencil of creamy-white hair extending to the basal third of the black tarsi. Expanse of wings 26 millim.

Samburu, 4th November, 1896.

Unfortunately only one slightly damaged example of this beautiful species was obtained [1].

216. ARNIOCERA CYANOXANTHA. (Plate XXXIII. fig. 5.)

♀. *Zygæna cyanoxantha*, Mabille, Ann. Soc. Ent. Belg. 1893, p. 57; Mabille and Vuillot, Novit. Lep. fasc. xii. p. 151, pl. xxi. fig. 6.

Samburu, 10th November, 1896.

One typical male differs from Mabille's figure in the loss of the orange spot below the subapical one : the other examples have all the spots brilliant crimson instead of orange : the name for the species is therefore not very characteristic. The specimens are not in specially good condition, so I hope Mr. Betton will obtain others.

217. ARNIOCERA IMPERIALIS, sp. n. (Plate XXXIII. fig. 6.)

♂. Primaries above shining Prussian green, changing to blue at outer margin, five black-edged carmine spots (the two central ones sometimes confluent, forming a transverse band) as in *A. cyano-xantha*, fringe purple flecked with copper : secondaries with the basi-costal half bright rose-colour, tinged with orange at base ; outer half bright Antwerp blue, changing to purple on the fringe ; an ill-defined subapical cluster of rosy scales : thorax glittering steely green, yellowish on centre of dorsum ; sides of face purple ; palpi carmine ; sides of collar and inner border of patagia crimson ; metathorax with sides and hind margin orange ; abdomen orange-vermilion, tinted with carmine at the sides, basal segment greenish black. Primaries below bright blue, spots as above, but more vermilion ; base of cell varied with golden testaceous : secondaries rose-red, with a basi-costal dash and a longitudinal costal streak blue ; a squamose blackish streak from end of cell to extremity of vein 1 ; fringe greyish coppery at apex : body below blue-black ; anterior coxæ orange-vermilion ; a golden line along inner edge of tibiæ ; middle tibiæ carmine with black tips ; posterior tibiæ with long cream-whitish pencil of hairs. Expanse of wings 32 millim.

Samburu, 10th November, 1896.

Two tolerably good examples of this lovely moth were obtained.

---

[1] The following beautiful new species was presented to the Museum by Dr. Edward A. Heath :—

ARNIOCERA ERICATA, sp. n. (Plate XXXIII. fig. 4.)

Primaries glossy greenish black ; a broad irregular subbasal belt, a bilobed oblique postmedian abbreviated band, and a large ovate oblique subapical patch scarlet : secondaries with ochreous costal area, otherwise the basal half vermilion, with an irregular submedian basal blue-black patch ; external half blue-black, throwing a long inner process up vein 1, enclosing a large scarlet subapical spot, and slightly sprinkled with scarlet along outer margin : thorax greenish black ; abdomen scarlet, transversely banded with indigo-blackish ; antennæ and palpi black ; anterior legs greenish black ; tibiæ slightly testaceous internally, tarsi with reddish short bristles ; middle legs with the femora greenish black, slightly chestnut below (possibly owing to abrasion) ; tibiæ clothed with scarlet hair, with tip and spurs black ; tarsi brown ; hind legs a good deal rubbed, but apparently similar to the middle pair : wings below nearly as above, but the primaries broadly orange at the base. Expanse of wings 34 millim.

British East Africa (*Heath*).

218. ARNIOCERA STERNECKI.  (Plate XXXIII. fig. 7.)

*Arichalca sternecki*, Rogenhofer in Baumann's Usambara u. s. Nachbargebiete, p. 331 (1891).

Maungu Inkubwa, 21st March, 1897.

Rogenhofer describes his insect as having the abdomen and secondaries yellow; in Mr. Betton's specimens they are carmine. Either the type was a faded specimen or one of those orange-yellow variations common among the crimson-winged *Zygænidæ*. The species is quite new to us.

## PYRALIDÆ.

219. ANCYLOLOMIA CHRYSOGRAPHELLUS.

*Crambus chrysographellus*, Kollar in Hügel's Kaschmir, p. 494.

Taru, 27th November, 1896.

220. BRIHASPA CHRYSOSTOMUS.

*Schœnobius chrysostomus*, Zeller, Micr. Caffr. p. 68.

Mgana, 1st & 9th August, 1896.

New to the collection from East Africa.

221. PATISSA sp.

Close to *P. fulvosparsa*, but without the ochreous markings; it has lost both labial palpi and fringes, and may even be a very worn example of the Asiatic species: therefore I hesitate about giving it a name.

Samburu, 4th November, 1896.

222. MACALLA sp.

Maungu Inkubwa, 3rd April, 1897.

One shattered female was obtained, but, even if perfect, it would not be satisfactory to describe it without seeing the male, the antennal characters of that sex often differing in species of the same genus.

223. LEPIDOGMA sp.

Taru, 24th November, 1896.

One slightly damaged female; it was enclosed in the same envelope with a much worn and quite unrecognizable Noctuid (apparently a *Metachrostis*). It is of no use to describe this species without its male; it and the preceding are both new to the Museum series, and will probably be of service when the other sex comes to hand.

224. ZITHA VARIANS, sp. n.   (Plate XXXIII. figs. 8, 9.)

Primaries vinaceous grey-brown or bright chestnut, with or without marginal dusky dots; a broad central belt, either more dusky or scarcely differing in tint from the ground-colour, but margined on both sides by more or less dentate-sinuate whitish stripes diverging on costal margin; the inner stripe more or less strongly inangulated below median vein, the outer stripe zigzag;

a whitish spot below base of cell; a series of white costal points
between the two transverse stripes; a more or less prominent
blackish reniform stigma; a whitish line at the base of the fringe :
secondaries paler than primaries, crossed beyond the middle by a
dusky bordered whitish line parallel to outer margin; a whitish
line at base of fringe : body darker than ground-colour of wings.
Under surface of wings paler and more uniform than above, reddish
on costal and outer borders, whitish on internal area; a dusky
median shade bounded by the outer whitish stripe of the primaries
and the postmedian whitish stripe of the secondaries; inner
whitish stripe of primaries obsolete; a blackish spot at the
anterior angle of each discoidal cell; indistinct dusky marginal
dots followed by the whitish line at base of fringe : body below
somewhat darker and redder than the wings, the tibiæ and tarsi
paler.   Expanse of wings 23 to 25 millim.

Voi, 17th April; between Voi and Ndi, 4th June, 1897.

### 225. PYCNARMON CRIBRATA.

*Phalæna cribrata*, Fabricius, Ent. Syst. iii. 2, p. 215 (1794).

Mgana, 12th August, 1896.

New to us from East Africa; indeed, we previously only
possessed one African example (from Sierra Leone).

### 226. LYGROPIA AMYNTUSALIS.

*Botys amyntusalis*, Walker, Cat. Lep. Het. xviii. p. 662 (1859).

Marago ya Fundi, 4th March, 1897.

The same observation applies to this as to the preceding species.

### 227. SYNGAMIA ABRUPTALIS.

*Asopia?* *abruptalis*, Walker, Cat. Lep. Het. xvii. p. 371 (1859).

Mgana, 5th August, 1896.

New to the Museum from Eastern Africa, though we have it
from Accra.

### 228. GLYPHODES STENOCRASPIS, sp. n.   (Plate XXXIII. fig. 10.)

Wings pearly semitransparent white; primaries with narrow
gilded brown costal border, very narrow darker brown outer
border excised below vein 8; fringe greyish brown, with slender
white basal line; a small black spot at end of cell : secondaries
with narrow dark brown border not reaching anal angle, fringe as
in primaries : body snow-white, the patagia silvery, the collar
slightly stained yellowish, front of forehead brownish testaceous;
anal tuft black : wings below nearly as above, but the borders
paler, costal border confined to the extreme margin and a stain
towards apex.   Expanse of wings 29 millim.

Mombasa, 4th January, 1897.

Nearest to the Western *G. elealis* Walk. (of which *Phakellura
peridromella* Mab. is a synonym), but with the brown borders to
the wings considerably narrower; the excision of the outer border
at apex of primaries also allies this species to *G. albifuscalis* Hamps.

229. GLYPHODES SINUATA.

*Phalæna sinuata*, Fabricius, Ent. Syst. iii. 2, p. 208 (1793).
Voi, 1st May, 1897.

230. LEPYRODES GEOMETRALIS.

*Lepyrodes geometralis*, Guenée, Delt. et Pyral. p. 278.
British E. Africa (no exact locality or date on envelope).
New to the Museum from Eastern Africa; we have it from Accra.

231. LEPYRODES CAPENSIS.

*Lepyrodes capensis*, Walker, Cat. Lep. Het. xxxiv. p. 1344 (1865).
Mgana, 1st August, 1896.
New to us from Eastern Africa.

232. ZEBRONIA PHENICE.

*Phalæna phenice*, Cramer, Pap. Exot. iv. p. 185, pl. ccclxxxii. G
(1782).
Mgana, 1st August, 1896; Mombasa, 4th January, 1897.
New to us from the Eastern coast; we have it from Uganda.

### TINEIDÆ.

233. MICROCOSSUS BETTONI, sp. n.

Nearest to *M. mackwoodi*: sordid sericeous white; primaries
transversely reticulated with brown lines, some of which are dotted
with black scales; the reticulated lines are coarser on costal
border, especially towards the base and the apex, and form the
boundaries of slightly brownish quadrate spots, the best defined
of these spots is placed on the costa just above the end of the
cell; antennæ bronze-brown, sericeous, with dull testaceous pectinations in the male: under surface brownish; primaries with ill-
defined darker brown patches. Expanse of wings 25 to 30 millim.
♂ ♀, Samburu, 31st October, 1896.
Only one pair of this obscure little moth was obtained, unfortunately not in perfect condition.

234. A Micro-Lepidopteron of doubtful genus.

Taru, 16th December, 1896; Voi, 2nd May, 1897.
A very beautiful little moth quite new to the Museum: the
primaries blue-green and glistening, the secondaries sericeous
purple; anterior half of body black, posterior half golden ochreous.
Not having paid much attention to the *Tineidæ* I will not pretend
to decide where this insect should be placed; it has antennæ
which remind one of typical *Zygænidæ*, and, so far as I remember,
are only approached by *Exodomorpha* or *Eretmocera*.

The following new genus, structurally, should be an Arctian,
and must therefore be placed in the *Arctiidæ*, but it has much
more nearly the aspect of a Noctuid of the *Plusia* group of
genera; it reminds one a little of *Culasta* and (in style of coloration) of *Rhynchina*.

### METACULASTA, gen. nov.

Primaries elongate, subtriangular; vein 2 remote from 3; 3, 4, and 5 separate but emitted near together; 6 from upper angle of cell, 7 from centre of postdiscoidal areole, 8 and 9 stalked, out of 10, which forms front of areole; 11 emitted well before end of cell: secondaries with costa slightly angular at centre; veins 2 to 6 as in primaries, 7 and 8 anastomosed to near end of cell: thorax broad, flattened above; head rather wide; antennæ smooth, palpi directed obliquely upwards; hind tibiæ with two pairs of spurs, inner spurs very long. Type *M. dives.*

235. METACULASTA DIVES, sp. n.

♀. Primaries above golden testaceous, longitudinally indistinctly streaked with greyish and flecked with blackish near the borders; a black dot at upper angle of cell; a very oblique shining silver streak towards the base, just entering the discoidal cell and not extending below vein 1; a second slightly-waved arched oblique streak commencing at about the basal third of inner margin (where it is indistinct) and extending to apex; a pale diffused flesh-tinted band runs above the latter, almost filling the interval between the two silver streaks on the lower half of the wing; fringe with a pale basal line: secondaries pearl-white, slightly buffish at costal and outer margins: thorax ash-greyish; abdomen whity brown, nearly white. Primaries below whity brown, showing traces of the upper surface markings through the wing: body below white; tarsi slightly brownish underneath. Expanse of wings 33 millim.

Voi, 11th July, 1897.

## EXPLANATION OF THE PLATES.

### PLATE XXXII.

Fig. 1. *Pyrgus bettoni*, p. 415.
2. *Baoris auritinctus*, p. 416.
3. *Aloa bivittata*, p. 417.
4. *Lacydes gracilis*, p. 417.
5. *Bettonia ferruginea*, p. 418.
6. *Lacipa impuncta*, p. 427.
7. *Lopera monosticta*, p. 428.
8. *Aclonophlebia flavinotata*, p. 428.
9. *Niphadolepis auricincta*, p. 437.
10. *Paryphanta bisecta*, p. 437.
11. *Lembopteris puella*, p. 438.
12. *Stauropus dasychiroides*, p. 433.
13. *Hamcopis rudicornis*, p. 435.

### PLATE XXXIII.

Fig. 1. *Goodia hollandi*, p. 430.
2. *Trotonotus bettoni*, p. 431.
3. *Arniocera chrysosticta*, p. 439.
4. " *ericata*, p. 440.
5. " *cyanoxantha*, var., p. 440.
6. " *imperialis*, p. 440.
7. " *sternecki*, var., p. 441.
8, 9. *Zitha varians*, p. 441.
10. *Glyphodes stenocraspis*, p. 442.